6/90

ABOUT THE AUTHOR

Barbara Cartland, the world's most famous romantic novelist, who is also an historian, playwright, lecturer, political speaker and television personality, has now written over 490 books and sold nearly 500 million copies all over the world.

She has also had many historical works published and has written four autobiographies as well as the biographies of her mother and that of her brother, Ronald Cartland, who was the first Member of Parliament to be killed in the last war. This book has a preface by Sir Winston Churchill and has just been republished with an introduction by the late Sir Arthur Bryant.

"Love at the Helm" a novel written with the help and inspiration of the late Earl Mountbatten of Burma, Great Uncle of His Royal Highness The Price of Wales, is being sold for the Mountbatten Memorial Trust.

She has broken the world record for the last thirteen years by writing an average of twenty-three books a year. In the Guinness Book of Records she is listed as the world's top-selling author.

Miss Cartland in 1978 sang an Album of Love Songs with the Royal Philharmonic Orchestra.

In private life Barbara Cartland, who is a Dame of Grace of the Order of St. John of Jerusalem, Chairman of the St. John Council in Hertfordshire and Deputy President of the St. John Ambulance Brigade, has fought for better conditions and salaries for Midwives and Nurses.

She championed the cause for the Elderly in 1956 invoking a Government Enquiry into the "Housing Conditions of Old People".

In 1962 she had the Law of England changed so that Local Authorities had to provide camps for their own Gypsies. This has meant that since then thousands and thousands of Gypsy children have been able to go to School which they had never been able to do in the past, as their caravans were moved every twenty-four hours by the Police.

There are now fourteen camps in Hertfordshire and Barbara Cartland has her own Romany Gypsy Camp called Barbaraville by the Gypsies.

Her designs "Decorating with Love" are being sold all over the U.S.A. and the National Home Fashions League made her, in 1981, "Woman of Achievement".

Barbara Cartland's book "Getting Older, Growing Younger" has been published in Great Britain and the U.S.A. and her fifth Cookery Book, "The Romance of Food", is now being used by the House of Commons.

In 1984 she received at Kennedy Airport, America's Bishop Wright Air Industry Award for her contribution to the development of aviation. In 1931 she and two R.A.F. Officers thought of, and carried the first aeroplane-towed glider air-mail.

During the War she was Chief Lady Welfare Officer in Bedfordshire looking after 20,000 Service men and women. She thought of having a pool of Wedding Dresses at the War Office so a Service Bride could hire a gown for the day.

She bought 1,000 gowns without coupons for the A.T.S., the W.A.A.F.s and the W.R.E.N.S. In 1945 Barbara Cartland received the Certificate of Merit from Eastern Command.

In 1964 Barbara Cartland founded the National Association for Health of which she is the President, as a front for all the Health Stores and for any product made as alternative medicine.

This has now a £500,000,000 turnover a year, with one third going in export.

In January 1988 she received "La Medaille de Vermeil de la Ville de Paris", (the Gold Medal of Paris). This is the highest award to be given by the City of Paris for ACHIEVEMENT — 25 million books sold in France.

In March 1988 Barbara Cartland was asked by the Indian

Government to open their Health Resort outside Delhi. This is almost the largest Health Resort in the world.

Barbara Cartland was received with great enthusiasm by her fans, who also fêted her at a Reception in the city and she received the gift of an embossed plate from the Government.

OTHER BOOKS BY BARBARA CARTLAND

Romantic Novels, over 490 the most recently published being:

Hidden by Love	The Dangerous Marriage
Walking to Wonderland	Good or Bad
Lucky Logan Finds Love	This is Love
Born of Love	Seek the Stars
The Angel and the Rake	Escape to Love
The Queen of Hearts	Look with the Heart
The Wicked Widow	Safe in Paradise
To Scotland and Love	Love in the Ruins
Love and War	Coronation of Love
Love at the Ritz	A Duel of Jewels

The Dream and the Glory (In aid of the St. John Ambulance Brigade)

Autobiographical and Biographical:

The Isthmus Years   1919-1939
The Years of Opportunity   1939-1945
I Search for Rainbows   1945-1976
We Danced All Night   1919-1929
Ronald Cartland (With a foreword by Sir Winston Churchill)
Polly — My Wonderful Mother
I Seek the Miraculous

Historical:

Bewitching Women

The Outrageous Queen (The Story of Queen Christina of Sweden)
The Scandalous Life of King Carol
The Private Life of Charles II
The Private Life of Elizabeth, Empress of Austria
Josephine, Empress of France
Diane de Poitiers
Metternich — The Passionate Diplomat
A Year of Royal Days

Sociology:

You in the Home	Etiquette
The Fascinating Forties	The Many Facets of Love
Marriage for Moderns	Sex and the Teenager
Be Vivid, Be Vital	The Book of Charm
Love, Life and Sex	Living Together
Vitamins for Vitality	The Youth Secret
Husbands and Wives	The Magic of Honey
Men and Wonderful	The Book of Beauty and
Women the Enigma	Health

Keep Young and Beautiful by Barbara Cartland and Elinor Glyn
Etiquette for Love and Romance
Barbara Cartland's Book of Health

Cookery:

Barbara Cartland's Health Food Cookery Book
Food for Love
Magic of Honey Cookbook
Recipes for Lovers
The Romance of Food

Editor of:

"The Common Problem" by Ronald Cartland (with a preface by the Rt. Hon. the Earl of Selborne, P.C.)

Barbara Cartland's Library of Love
                    Library of Ancient Wisdom

"Written with Love" Passionate love letters selected by
Barbara Cartland

Drama:

Blood Money
French Dressing

Philosophy:

Touch the Stars

Radio Operetta:

The Rose and the Violet (Music by Mark Lubbock)
Performed in 1942.

Radio Plays:

The Caged Bird: An episode in the life of Elizabeth
Empress of Austria Performed in 1957.

General:

Barbara Cartland's Book of Useless Information with a
Foreword by the Earl Mountbatten of Burma.
(In aid of the United World Colleges)

Love and Lovers   (Picture Book)

The Light of Love   (Prayer Book)

Barbara Cartland's Scrapbook
(In aid of the Royal Photographic Museum)

Romantic Royal Marriages

Barbara Cartland's Book of Celebrities

Getting Older, Growing Younger

Verse:

Lines on Life and Love

Music:

An Album of Love Songs sung with the Royal Philharmonic Orchestra.

Films:

The Flame is Love
A Hazard of Hearts
The Lady and The Highwayman

Cartoons:

Barbara Cartland Romances (Book of Cartoons) has recently been published in the U.S.A., Great Britain, and other parts of the world.

Children:

A Children's Pop-Up Book: "Princess to the Rescue"

Videos:

A Hazard of Hearts
The Lady and The Highwayman

"ROYAL LOVERS"

BY

BARBARA CARTLAND

This book required an enormous
amount of research and I am
deeply grateful for the untiring
help of Bea Cayzer, Audrey Elliott,
Hazel Clark, and Sally Barnes.

Drawings by Roger Hall and
Trefor Salter.

"ROYAL LOVERS"

ISBN 0 905377 43 5

First Publication in Great Britain

Copyright © 1989 Cartland Promotions

Published by
Marwain Publishing Limited
Marwain House
Clarke Road
Mount Farm
Milton Keynes
MK1 1LG

Typeset by
Grillford Limited, Granby, Milton Keynes

Printed and bound by
Richard Clay, Bungay, Suffolk

CONTENTS

*H.R.H. PRINCE ALEXANDER OF HESSE AND
JULIE VON HAUKE*

H.R.H. PRINCE ALEXANDER OF HESSE AND THE RHINE AND JULIE VON HAUKE

Prince Alexander of Hesse left his Father's Palace at Darmstadt to live in St. Petersburg with his sister Marie who at sixteen had married the Tzarevitch — the future Tzar Alexander II.

On the day of his Christening Alexander, who was a Godson of the Tzar, had been made a Lieutenant in the Russian Imperial Army. When he reached St. Petersburg he was promoted to Major General.

He was a brilliant, dashing, extremely brave soldier, who was a volunteer in the expedition to put down a rebellion in the Caucasus, led by the Modammedan Shamyl.

He won the Order of St. George for valour and scooped a nice souvenir off the littered battlefield — the late Shamyl's own Koran.

Back at Court he fell wildly in love with his sister's new and very pretty Polish Lady-in-Waiting, Julie Hauke.

She was an orphan, because her aristocratic mother had died young, and her father Maurice, General of Artillery in the Imperial Russian Army, and Minister of War in the satellite government of Poland, had been killed defending the Palace in Warsaw against rebellious Polish cadets in 1830.

He died saving the life of the Governor General of Poland, Grand Duke Constantine, brother of the Tsar.

The latter gratefully brought up General Hauke's two orphaned daughters in his own household, which is how Julie happened to move in such exalted circles.

Julie was a remarkably pretty girl with dark brown hair, her mouth was small and sweet, and her large brown eyes were warm and wistful.

Prince Alexander was in 1851, very close to the pinnacle of Russian Military importance and the Tzar told him he was going to give him an even greater honour than he had previously.

Alexander waited expectantly, and was appalled when the Tzar told him he was giving him his niece in marriage the Grand Duchess Catherine Michailova.

The Prince was horrified but did not dare to say that he refused. He searched out Julie and told her what had been planned.

She burst into tears, clung to him and he knew in that moment that there was only one thing they could do and that was to elope.

At midnight they dashed in a droshky drawn by three horses from Tsarkoie-Selo. the Summer Palace, to St. Petersburg.

Then they rattled in a wood-burning train over the endless flat plains of Western Russia and Poland, eventually crossing the Russian border to Breslau.

Here on the 28th October 1851 they were married by a nervous priest.

They then telegraphed the news to their august relatives in Peterhof.

Tzar Nicholas was furious.

He stripped Alexander of his Military rank and threw him out of the Imperial Russian Army.

Fortunately for the Prince, his brother, now Grand Duke Louis III reigned in Hesse-Darmstadt. The marriage was morganatic, but Julie had to have a name.

The Grand Duke discovered a lapsed and forgotten title for his new sister-in-law. He created her Countess of Battenberg.

Seven years later when she had given Prince Alexander several good-looking sons and a beautiful daughter, she became Her Serene Highness, The Princess of Battenberg and her children had the same rank.

This, although neither she nor her gallant husband — who had achieved more honours in battle and more Orders — were aware of it, was the beginning of a great and glorious Royal Family from Battenberg to Mountbatten.

PRINCE CLEMENT METTERNICH AND H.R.H. PRINCESS KATHARINA BAGRATION

One of the most attractive, charming and intelligent men that ever walked the world was Prince Metternich.

He was known among his contemporaries as 'The Passionate Diplomat' and he was adored by almost every woman he met who lost her heart from the moment he spoke to her.

His charm, as well as his brilliance vibrated all over Europe and every year he rose higher and higher in the Diplomatic Service.

One morning the Imperial Minister was sitting in the garden of his Legation cutting his quill pen when he heard the sound of a carriage drawing up before the entrance to the Palace.

The sound of someone fiercely ringing the bell came to his ears.

A footman rushed to open the door.

The ringing was so imperative that Clement Metternich rose from his chair and went into the corridor to see what was happening.

He expected to find one of the Imperial Couriers, a bully who was ever conscious of his importance, standing in the sunlight against the dark hallway.

Instead, to his astonishment he saw standing there in transparent loveliness the most exquisite figure he had ever seen.

The lady was dressed in the latest fashion of the *directoire*.

Her gown was so thin that her body, like a beautiful marble statue, shone through the diaphanous material.

Prince Metternich stood for a moment enchanted by the picture she made.

It seemed to him that he was intentionally delaying inviting the vision to enter that he might keep her beauty for ever in his mind.

As he walked nearer to her he saw a child-like face, white as alabaster, with rose-tinted cheeks, delicate features and eyes that seemed shy and helpless.

He was never to forget the first visit to his Palace of Princess Katharina Bagration.

He described it to a colleague many years later, by saying:

"There was Oriental softness about her, Andalusian grace and Parisian elegance. She was like a beautiful naked angel!"

As he said the last words his voice dropped to a whisper and his eyes seemed to cloud with the memory of what he had seen and felt that day.

The Prince was so impressed with the beauty of his visitor that he forgot to beg permission to change his clothing.

He was wearing a silk shirt and a purple velvet dressing-gown trimmed with sable.

Princess Katharina, in describing him, said:

"He was Apollo descended upon earth!"

The meeting of these two young people, so handsome, beautiful and so mutually appreciative inevitably had significant results.

Princess Bagration was a direct descendant of the brother of Katharina I of Russia and on her mother's side a niece of the Chancellor Prince Potemkin.

Her husband, Prince Peter Bagration was a General in the Tsar's Armies, and old enough to be her father.

It was a curious chain of circumstances that threw these two people together in the Legation at Dresden.

Kotzebue, the Dramatist who had satirized the two Metternichs in his Play *"The Two Klingsbergs"* had become an Agent in the Imperial Russian Secret Service.

When he heard of Clement Metternich's appointment to the Court of the Elector of Saxony, he immediately notified his superiors.

The young Minister, Kotzebue had reported, was

married to the granddaughter of the great Chancellor Prince Kaunitz, and therefore related to the most important families of the empire.

He was young, brilliant and easy-going.

Moreover, in the opinion of Kotzebue, he would prove an easy victim of the lovely and intelligent young lady whom the Russian Government might select to bedazzle him.

Tsar Alexander, the new Russian Emperor, had abandoned the policy of his father in flirting with the French cause, and now definitely was turning towards Vienna.

He had begun to feel the power of the Corsican Conqueror.

Austria was the only hope of successfully rising the tide of French domination.

The Russian Ambassador to Vienna had spoken highly of the great expectations entertained there for the Diplomatic career of Prince Metternich.

Tsar Alexander had therefore decided to send his most beautiful and skilled Agent to ingratiate herself into his favour.

Behind the Princess's appearance of bashful timidity was an extremely astute brain and her experience had won her recognition in the Russian Foreign Office as its most skilled Agent.

This was the young lady who was to be thrown at the head of the young Imperial Minister.

After the first shock of surprise they both felt at the sight of each other, the Princess recovered herself sufficiently to give her name and ask if she might see the Princess Eleanora Metternich.

Clement courteously informed her that his wife would not come to Dresden for another month, but that he would be pleased to entertain Her Highness in her absence.

He detected a note of relief in her face as he escorted her to the Salon where he ordered refreshments and assured her that he was at her disposal.

The attraction between them was so powerful that their first interview was by no means devoted entirely to matters of state.

They had both fallen in love and while their conversation dealt with the superficialities and gossip of the day, each was aware that the mask of nonchalance must eventually be cast aside.

In this respect Metternich had no qualms of conscience.

His wife adored him and she was so grateful to be in his life that she never reproached him for his many affairs.

She knew it was impossible for him not to attract women and she left him free to be himself.

Within a few weeks, all Dresden knew of the deep attachment which had grown up between the Imperial Minister from Vienna and Princess Katharina Bagration.

They appeared together at various Salons and everyone declared that they were the most handsome couple that had ever been seen.

The only dissenting voice in the chorus of adoration was that of Wilhelmina of Kurland, whose lovely eyes had followed the young Minister since his first appearance at a Salon.

The arrival of his wife at the Imperial Legation did not change in any way Prince Metternich's infatuation.

Indeed, a friendship sprang up between Eleanora and her husband's great friend, the French Minister, the *Marquis* de Mopustier.

Even though she knew that she was as free to follow her wishes as her husband, Eleanora would go no farther than friendship as far as the *Marquis* was concerned.

He was greatly impressed by her loyalty to Clement, and remained on the most intimate terms with both husband and wife.

Clement and Katharina were sitting in the *Boudoir* of her house which was one of the most exquisitely furnished in the Saxon Capital.

They had dined together and now as they talked, they sipped slowly of the excellent liqueurs which the servants had left before leaving them alone.

"You are right, Clement," Katharina said decisively, "Russia and Austria must come together."

Katharina, ravishing in filmy pink lingerie, had been sitting on the arm of his chair.

He sat, staring absently into his tiny liqueur glass.

She was silent and he turned his head to look at her.

She was staring down at him, her arm resting on his shoulder.

The pupils of her eyes suddenly became larger as if they covered almost the entire iris.

He saw the look of longing that had stolen over her features.

Suddenly she seized his face and kissed his lips passionately.

He took her into his arms and lifted her onto his lap.

Intrigue was forgotten as they clung to each other and thought only of themselves and their love.

Later they drank to the future of Austria.

Henceforth they were to be allies, not alone in love, but in politics as well.

Nearly every morning they could be seen riding together in the Englische Garten, near which Princess Bagration's house was situated.

Both were magnificent riders and together made a charming picture.

Nearly a year passed before one day Wilhelmina of Kurland who had never lost her infatuation for the young Envoy saw him riding alone in the English Garden, the Princess no longer beside her lover.

Wilhelmina, who was extremely attractive, joined him.

There were other times when Katharina was to be seen driving slowly along in her carriage, while the Austrian Minister rode beside her talking animatedly.

In the year 1802, Katharina gave birth to a daughter.

There is no record as to Tsar Alexander's reception of the news that his most capable Agent had been so blessed.

Prince Bagration had not seen his wife for three years.

The baby was given the legitimate name of Prince Peter, but the child's given name was Clementine, after the Imperial Austrian Minister.

Prince Peter made no objection for he had neglected his wife scandalously, and a female infant anyway could have no hereditary claim upon his properties.

It was at this point that Eleanora came to the assistance of her husband.

She suggested they should bring up the child and she said:

"You may be sure, Clement, that I will give it the same affection I would bestow upon our own."

And so the tiny Princess Clementine Bagration entered the Metternich household.

There was only one person in all Dresden who objected to the affair between Prince Metternich and the Princess and its outcome and that was Wilhelmina of Kurland, who was more infuriated than any wife could have been.

She instantly left Dresden for Berlin, where she married the Prince Rohan.

The affair between Prince Metternich and Princess Katharina did not break off with the arrival of the infant.

Their affection endured throughout their lives, although later upon less intimate terms.

Years later, when Katharina was an elderly lady and Metternich had lost that youthful charm, that had first attracted her to him, he still remained the greatest love of her life.

Whenever she came to see him she wore a filmy dress which had been especially made for her in the *directoire* fashion.

She wanted to appear as near as possible to the exquisite girl who had first stood silhouetted in the sunshine against the dark arch of the Austrian Legation.

And had looked like 'a beautiful, naked angel'.

H.R.H. PRINCESS BAGRATION

PRINCE METTERNICH

DAISY BROOKE

KING EDWARD VII

KING EDWARD VII AND LADY BROOKE.
1841-1910.

Brilliant in his understanding of people and a peacemaker, King Edward VII was also very sensuous and debonair.

Somebody wrote of Edward, Prince of Wales, and it was true:

"He had a charm that was irresistable and he also loved beautiful women."

Loved was the right word.

When he took a woman as his mistress, because he loved her passionately and with his heart, he also respected her.

Kings have had mistresses since the beginning of time, but Edward VII as Prince of Wales, and as King, made it possible for the first time, for a Gentleman to have an *affaire-de-coeur* with a woman of his own class.

Previously, every social door was shut against any woman who had the slightest breath of scandal spread about her or in any way was suspected of being improper.

This changed with the advent of the breath-takingly beautiful Lilie Langtry.

In 1875 Benjamin Disraeli received an interesting report from his Secretary, who was a guest at Easton Lodge.

He wrote:

"The Heiress Miss Daisy is growing into a fine young woman. She is now fifteen, so that she will not for three years be the talk of London. Munster says her fortune will be much over £30,000 a year. Whatever it be, I see she will bestow it upon whosoever she chooses — and turn out a maitresse femme."

The following year, Daisy Maynard was noticed by Lord Brooke, the eldest son of the Earl of Warwick.

He fell in love at first sight, but when he asked Daisy's stepfather, Lord Rosslyn, if he might mention this to Daisy, the answer was a stern 'No'.

Her mother, Lady Rosslyn had great ambitions for her eldest daughter.

Queen Victoria, the 'Matchmaker of Europe'. had recently decided that it was uneconomic to keep marrying off her children to penniless German Royalties, who invariably needed large settlements.

She had chosen Lord Lorne, son of the Duke of Argyll for Princess Louise.

She was now considering an English Heiress for her youngest son, Prince Leopold, the Duke of Albany.

Descriptions of Daisy Maynard aroused the Queen's interest.

Daisy's mother Lady Rosslyn was delighted.

It would certainly be a great match.

In December 1879, Lord and Lady Rosslyn were commanded to bring Daisy to Windsor Castle.

She had not yet been presented at Court.

After dinner, Queen Victoria asked her a few questions.

Daisy Warwick said later:

"I was agonisingly shy in the presence of the mysterious Queen, but self-consciousness was my usual state of mind in those days."

For her eighteenth birthday a dance was held at Easton Lodge and Lord Brooke was grateful to receive an invitation.

He was made, however, to promise not to propose marriage by reiterating his hopes.

The following Spring, Daisy was enjoying her first Season.

Queen Victoria and Lady Rosslyn brought marriage negotiations to a climax.

Daisy was invited to stay at Prince Leopold's country house, and there the eighteen-year-old girl firmly refused his offer.

A few hours later, while walking under an umbrella with the Equerry Lord Brooke, she accepted the second marriage proposal of the day.

Queen Victoria was displeased.

Daisy was married and extremely happy with Lord Brooke, who was a charming, easy-going and very popular young man.

She was an excellent hostess and they gave large parties, where she liked to pick her own guests, chose her own meals and enjoy the company of her numerous animals.

During the early years of their marriage, the names of Lord and Lady Beresford often appeared on the Easton Lodge visitors' book.

Lord Charles had made his name in Naval combat and it was inevitable therefore that Daisy should admire him as a hero.

She also found him outstandingly attractive as a man.

Within five years of her marriage, Daisy was gazing with undisguised admiration at the splendid reckless sailor who was a close friend of the Prince of Wales.

In 1884 Lord Charles was away in Egypt, organising the transport steamers through the Nile cataracts to relieve General Gordon at Khartoum.

After the Battle of Abu Klea, at which all the Naval Officers except Beresford were killed, he agreed with a comrade that it would 'be indeed hard to die without knowing who had won the Derby'.

He then managed to rescue Sir Charles Wilson's advance detachment left in isolation after Khartoum fell, and this dangerous operation, brilliantly performed under enemy fire, won him the C.B.

In July 1885, the hero returned.

Daisy Brooke, who like a diligent wife, was producing her third child, gave a celebration of fireworks at Easton Lodge to the amazement of the villagers and the delight of the County.

Five months later, when her child was born, the Brookes named him Charles.

Unfortunately the little boy died in infancy and it was thirteen years before Daisy had another baby.

During that period she was to have a disastrous quarrel with Lord Charles Beresford.

Daisy was reckless as well as beautiful.

When she was in love she threw caution to the winds.

She discovered that at the age of forty Lady Charles Beresford, who had produced a daughter over ten years before, was pregnant.

Daisy went wild with fury.

Charles Beresford had sworn to be true to her and like an outraged child, Daisy accused him of infidelity!

Tears, tantrums, smelling-salts, nothing could persuade her that Charlie had not behaved disgracefully.

In January 1889. Lady Beresford claimed that her husband had told her to open his mail.

She had therefore opened a letter addressed to him written in a well-known flowing hand.

The Prime Minister the Marquess of Salisbury, a day later, received a furious letter from Lady Charles.

She explained how she had opened Lady Brooke's letter saying that in it she read:

"Mina had no right to have your child!"

When Lord Charles returned to London Lady Beresford did not tell him that she had intercepted Daisy's letter.

She placed it in the care of Mr. Lewis, the well-known Solicitor.

She merely asked her husband to take her to the South of France for 'health's sake'.

The Beresfords lived only two miles from Lady Brooke's Villa on the Riviera.

It was not until she returned to London that Daisy Brooke was notified by the Solicitor that he held her most damaging letter.

She was bewildered and shocked and Daisy could obviously not turn to her husband for help.

As the Prince and Princess of Wales had often stayed at Easton Lodge and she had thought him very affable, she thought that he might be able to help her.

After all, the Prince was Charlie Beresford's great friend and he might be able to retrieve the letter which she now very much regretted having written.

Looking prettier than ever, if flustered, Daisy called at Marlborough House.

She poured out her woes to the Prince and begged him almost on her knees to help her.

Helping his friends was something that the Prince enjoyed doing, especially when they were in a tight corner.

The Prince drove after midnight to the house of Mr. Lewis, who taken aback at finding the Heir to the Throne on his doorstep took the unprofessional step of showing His Royal Highness the letter.

The Prince expressed surprise, but continued in his efforts.

He called on Lady Charles begging her to surrender the letter to him.

Lady Charles, however, recognised his uneasiness and realised her power.

What she wanted was to destroy Lady Brooke's position in Society.

A second call from the Prince merely incited her to go further.

The Prince of Wales then hinted that if Lady Charles kept this letter, he could no longer invite her to Marlborough House and her own position in London Society would be imperilled.

In a hysterical letter to Lord Salisbury, Lady Charles suggested that the Prince must be *'under the influence of the lady'*, for *'he was anything but concillatory to me. I still of course, undeterred by these threats, refused to return the letter for obvious reasons.''*

The Prince, somewhat annoyed at his failure, had to inform Lady Brooke that he had failed in his mission.

Her vivid blue eyes, filled with tears, appeared more seductive than ever.

As she wept on the Prince's shoulder, he found himself

falling deeply in love.

He was not just attracted. He was moved with an emotion which came from his heart and his feelings were more intense than he had ever known them to be before.

During this drama Lady Charles produced a baby which was a girl, then returned to the Social World to discover she was being left out of all the best parties.

Lord Charles was on his way to join the Cruiser *Undaunted,* but before leaving he called on Daisy Brooke.

To his annoyance, he found the Prince of Wales in her *Boudoir*.

There was a jealous scene during which there was a push and the Prince sat down heavily and unceremoniously on a sofa.

This was *lese-majeste,* as Charles Beresford was well aware.

He went off to sea, angry with himself, Daisy, Mina his wife, and the Prince.

Daisy Brooke now found herself in a new situation and could hardly not enjoy such complete supremacy over her enemy.

In the Racing Season she travelled with the Prince in his special train and sat looking fabulous in the Royal Box.

The Prince started to spend the weekends at Easton Lodge and the great houses were requested always to invite Lord and Lady Brooke when the Prince was expected to stay with them.

It was all wildly enjoyable and Lord Brooke took it all in very good part.

He had always found it difficult to be cross with his lovely wife for long.

In fact, he told one of his friends:

"I would rather be married to Daisy, with all her peccadilloes than to any other woman in the world, however virtuous."

The Prince's love for Daisy increased year by year.

His letters to her always began:

"My own adored little Daisy wifey. . ."

She undoubtedly meant more to him than any other woman he had ever met and for nine years, sensual though he was, no one else attracted him.

She was of course, in many ways unique.

Elinor Glyn, the famous novelist wrote:

"No one who ever stayed at Easton ever forgot their hostess, and most of them fell helplessly in love with her. In my long life, spent in so many different countries, and during which I have seen most of the beautiful women of the world, from film-stars to Queens, I have never seen one who was so completely fascinating as Daisy Brooke.

She would sail in from her own wing, carrying her piping bull-finch, her lovely eyes smiling with the merry innocent expression of a Persian kitten, that has just tangled a ball of silk. Hers was that supreme personal charm which I later described as 'It' because it is quite indefinable, and does not depend upon beauty or wit, although she possessed both in the highest degree. She was never jealous or spiteful to other women, and if she liked you she was the truest, most understanding friend."

Needless to say, the Prince and Daisy, in the nine years they were so close to each other, ran into difficulties, troubles and disturbances.

Many people tried to break them up in some way, but even when the passion between them had worn off, there was still the love in the Prince's heart which could never be quenched.

When, after thirteen years. Daisy Brooke found she was going to have a child by a man she loved almost disastrously, the Prince of Wales was not jealous.

He realised the affair was over and when she wrote hoping she could keep his friendship and that her enemies had not turned the Princess against her, H.R.H. replied:

"My own lovely little Daisy . . . She really quite forgives and condones the past, as I have corroborated what you

wrote of our friendship having been platonic for some years. You could not help, my loved one, writing to me as you did — though it gave me a pang after the letters I have received from you for nearly nine years! But I think I could read 'between the lines' everything you wished to convey. . .

The end of your beautiful letter touched me more than anything — but how could you, my loved one, imagine that I should withdraw my friendship with you? On the contrary I want to befriend you more than ever . . . Though our interests, as you have said, lie apart, still we have the sentimental feeling of affinity which cannot be eradicated by time.''

SULTAN ABDUL HAMID AND
AIMEE DUBUCQ DE RIVERY.
1784.

On her way home to Martinique from her Convent School in Nantes in France, Aimee Dubucq was captured by Algerian corsairs.

Almost before she was aware of the horror that had befallen her she was on her way to Constantinople as a present from the Dey of Algiers to his master, the Sultan of Turkey, Allah's Shadow upon Earth.

A beautiful, intelligent, pious and charming young woman, she had been a special favourite with the Nuns in the convent. There had been tears when she had set sail, and even the Mother Superior had been on the jetty to wave her farewell.

The terror she had felt aboard the ship that carried her to Constantinople was intensified when her arrival Aimee saw the enormous figure of the Chief Black Eunuch, a princely Nubian, waddling towards her, his ermine-lined pelisse swept out behind him, and his turban nodded with flamingo plumes.

He had come to the Gate of Felicity to inspect the Dey's offering to his Sublime master.

Beside him Aimee saw a great pyramid of heads — some so recently severed they reeked and steamed with blood. For a moment she thought she was in a nightmare, then as her large blue eyes realised what she was seeing was real, she fainted.

Because of her fair hair from her Norman ancestors, she was known in the harem as 'Naksh', 'The Beautiful One'. She was educated in the seductive arts of love in the Academie de l'Armour.

She spent hours lolling in Turkish baths, naked with the other odalisques, ladling perfumed water over each other, twisting peacock-feathers and jewels in their long hair, nibbling sugary comfits, idling away the hours.

Slowly Aimee began to adjust herself, and her sharp little French brain began to plan her future. The Chief Black Eunuch Kizlar Aga, who was her master, was her only hope because he was a man.

It was doubtful if she knew, or even sensed, that the history of the Ottoman Empire, was a long testimony to the enormous power yielded by women in the Harem.

The Sultan's visits to his odalisques were announced by eunuchs who rang a large gold bell. Then there was a frantic rush for their grandest clothes, and most brilliant maquillage.

Then they fluttered around the Sultan, hundreds of charmers each yearning for a chance to charm. He should have been the happiest of men! No competition, no rebuffs, all of them hanging on his words, applauding his every quip.

Whilst the caged nightingales outvied with each other, the perfumed breezes of the burning incense wafted through the pavilions, and overall, unseen but powerful, brooded the reassuring presence of the Court abortionist.

Sometimes the Sultan would take a malicious pleasure in ending the revels abruptly by stalking out in a temper, in which case there were reproaches, nerve storms, tears, dramas and extra doses of Opium all round.

The Sultan was a cultured voluptuary, a patriarchal figure with an enormous charm Aimee had not expected.

She dressed on the first occassion in unparalleled grandeur. She wore a tiny, pill-box hat laden with jewels her long hair falling to her waist powdered with diamonds which trembled amongst the gold and seemed to be scattered carefully, but were in fact cunningly attached by fine gold chains.

Before Aimee had arrived at this point, when the Kizlar Aga announced she was singled out for the Royal Alcove, she resisted with violence. She had carefully planned her line of conduct, but it is likely she had not envisaged this decisive moment with all its implications.

She realised there was no other way for her to obtain power but her reaction was that of a young, convent-bred girl, terrified of her fate.

With all her strategies and through commonsense, this outburst was uncontrollable, and the Kizlar Aga had never seen such a display of resistance. Aimee's fury made him fear she might not only be unco-operative, but downright dangerous.

The more she stormed, screamed, stamped her feet, the more the other odalisques regarded her with astonishment. Aimee was so difficult that he asked help from an old friend, the Circassian Kadine.

She was clever enough to play on the French girl's good sense, her emotion and her vanity.

Aimee had a practical side to her character. There were no more rebellious outbreaks, and in triumph the Chief Eunuch, Son Altesse Noir, conducted Mlle Dubucq de Rivery, to the Sultan Abd Ul Hamid I.

The Sultan found her blonde beauty, her Western intellect, and her French background fascinating. Surprisingly quickly she became his favourite.

In the secrecy of his bedroom the Sultan called her — 'The Golden Nightingale' because of her fair hair, 'Jewel of the Orient', 'Pearl of Delight', and 'Perfume of the Rose'.

At first Aimee responded with the names she had been taught to say:

"Oh, Master of Masters', 'Shadow of Allah upon the Earth', and 'Chosen Among the Chosen'."

Finally, like any little French girl responding to her lover, she said in her soft voice what the Sultan wanted to hear:

"I love you. I love you."

On the 20th July 1785, their son Mahmoud was born, and there was wild rejoicing for the baby was third in succession to the throne.

Because she presented the Sultan with a son, Aimee was now a Kadine. Kadines who had sons were at once placed in the highest ranks of hierarchy. All of them lived in hope of seeing their son as Sultan, themselves as Valideh Sultan.

There was no question that the Sultan was delighted with Aimee's child and with Aimee herself. He ordered a magnificent fete, with fireworks, wrestling matches and a pavilion made entirely of spun-sugar, decorated with palms.

Every year Aimee became more and more powerful. It was whispered that she converted the Sultan to Catholicism, and as she was passionately faithful to her religion there can be little doubt that she married him secretly according to its rights.

She behaved like a wife and the Sultan treated her like one, consulting her on the policy of the Ottoman Empire, until she was in the position to alter and direct it.

Aimee was in the Seraglio, yet she had always retained the fresh, silvery beauty of her Norman ancestry. She succeeded in imposing Western nursery restraints, along with certain hygienic and dietetic measures for the Harem for her child.

She could never return to France, but she was slowly contriving within the Ottoman Empire, a breach through which the Western air would one day pour. She spoke French with Mahmoud in secret, and as he grew older, she taught him the legends of France, the high deeds of Charlemagne and Le Vert Galant. The little Prince must have lisped the fables of La Fontaine.

It was profound love for all things French or Western, that was to remain with him all his life. The formation of his character was Western, and behind all his most decisive actions there was the little French girl from Martinique.

In the years to come, Aimee Dubucq de Rivery was to become one of the greatest powers of the Ottoman Empire, and her son Mahmoud became the great 'Reformer', the Sultan who brought Turkey from the past into the future.

He owed his great position and his great reputation entirely to his mother − Naksh, the beautiful one, the powerful one, who died in Seraglio where she had lived after entering it 33 years before.

AIMEE DUBUCQ

EMPEROR NAPOLEON III

EMPEROR NAPOLEON III AND HARRIET HOWARD.

Prince Louis Napoleon, in the summer of 1847 looked across Lady Blessington's Drawing-Room at the most beautiful and exquisite girl.

Their eyes met and it was impossible for either of them to look away.

They fell wildly and passionately in love at first sight.

The Prince was notorious for his fiery *affairs de coeur* and Harriet Howard was no innocent virgin.

Her parents were the owners of the Castle Hotel in Brighton and she had already run away with a Jockey to live as his mistress in London.

When she was eighteen her Protector passed her on to a certain Major Martyn who set her up in a great house surrounded by servants and horses.

He also placed a large fortune at her disposal.

When she met Louis Napoleon, Harriet gave her whole heart to him and taking her illegitimate son with her, she moved into an establishment in Berkeley Street.

She pretended it was a Lodging-House, but which had only one guest — Louis Napoleon.

She also kept open house for his fellow conspirators who constantly travelled to France on secret missions, bribing and subverting Army Officers.

They appeared among the poor in an effort to impress them with Louis Napoleon's generosity.

Harriet was twenty-three when she fell in love with Louis Napoleon and he was thirty-nine.

She was intelligent, energetic, dignified and discreet, a perfect companion for a politically ambitious man.

In 1848 in Europe there were wild street riots and revolutions.

One of them toppled the throne of Louis-Phillipe and obliged him to flee the Tuileries in a Hackney cab.

With astonishing speed a strong Bonaparte Party formed in France and Louis Napoleon found himself elected by the people of Paris to represent them in the National Assembly.

By the end of the year, against the ferocious opposition of partisan Frenchmen, he had become the President of France.

He took up residence in the Élyseès Palace where there was a garden door leading onto the Rue du Cirque where Harriet Howard was installed with her three boys and Louis Phillipe's dog which she had agreed to bring with her.

As in London, she contrived discreet dinner-parties with important people for Louis Napoleon, and presided over the smoke-filled rooms, where his friends, supporters and conspirators gathered to map out his political strategy.

The French people seeing Harriet Howard riding in the Bois with her three boys viewed her on the whole with approval.

"Who says our Prince-President is a fool?" they asked. "He has brought back from England the best horses and most beautiful woman."

Harriet was behaving herself with superb good manners.

At the same time, her position was an uneasy one.

While she received in the Rue Du Cirque the most influential people in France, the 'best people' did not even recognise her existence.

Harriet had refused to establish her social position as was usual by a marriage of convenience.

This was because she wished to be free to assume one day the supreme position as official mistress of the Emperor.

The all-powerful Princess Mathilde, who was Louis Napoleon's Cousin was known to express confidentially that she thought 'Miss Howard's ambition was to wear the diadem of an Empress.'

That was the great game on which all the conspirators had staked their hopes and Harriet's fortune for the restoration of the Empire.

Louis Napoleon spent much of his Presidential term campaigning in the Provinces.

Harriet, still unobtrusive, but close to him, sometimes followed him about in a cart dressed as a peasant.

She devised a crest for her carriage — the head of a horse.

She appeared in the Prince's Theatre-box covered in diamonds.

Louis Napoleon was too honourable to reproach her.

His term as President was coming to a close and any day now he might have to ask Harriet for her diamonds.

She had already made over to him her rich Italian properties on which he was able to obtain mortgages.

In the year 1852 she placed at his disposal all her liquid assets, including her jewels.

It is believed that it was Harriet's money that paid for the drums of all the Regiments in France to be slashed so that no call to arms could be sounded on the 2nd December.

That was the day by a *coup d'etat*. Louis Napoleon overthrew the Republican Government.

The following day he was in the Tuileries, Napoleon III Emperor of the French.

Harriet Howard was by his side.

For the next seventeen years Napoleon, a gentle and courtly man, reigned and never maliciously hurt anyone.

He was, however, a born conspirator and deception was built into his being.

No sooner had he become Emperor than his 'dear and faithful Harriet' was appalled to learn that he intended to marry Eugenie of Spain.

Louis Napoleon had tried a number of Royal brides only to be turned down one after another.

Harriet had been prepared to accept her lover's marriage to a *Royal* bride, but to be thrust aside and be cheated of a crown by a woman whose grandfather was as plebeian as her own, was intolerable.

Napoleon had, of course, not deprived himself of Harriet's love for Eugenie's sake any more than he deprived himself of any other love for Harriet's.

He spent tender nights with her, soothed her fears and kissed her tears away.

But she was beginning to bore him with her accusations of false and broken promises.

She wrote to a friend:

"His Majesty was here last night offering to pay me off; yes an Earldom in my own right, a Castle, and a decent French husband into the bargain . . . Oh! the pity of it all! I could put up with a dose of laudanum . . . The Lord Almighty spent two hours arguing with me . . . Later he fell asleep on the crimson sofa and snored while I wept."

Napoleon was not niggardly, especially to the women he loved.

He was to recompense Harriet not only with the return of her own estate, but with hard cash the equivalent of four million dollars.

She accepted the title of The Countess of Beauregard and for a while she had the happiness of receiving her lover back into her arms, especially on those occasions when Eugenie locked him out of her bedroom.

The Emperor would start out for Beauregard driving in his coach dressed in Martial splendour.

On the way he would take off his star-studded coat and don a civilian jacket over his imperial trousers.

By the time he greeted Harriet, at least the upper half of him was a plain Prince-President, just as in the heyday of their love.

KING FRANÇOIS I OF FRANCE AND FRANÇOISE DE CHATEAUBRIANT

1494-1547.

One of François's most famous mistresses was Françoise de Chateaubriant, who was married to Jean Laval at the age of eleven and gave birth to a child a year later.

Ten years afterwards King François heard about this beauty who lived with her husband in a Château in Brittany.

He decided to invite them both to Blois.

The Court led a roving life in those days, but the King's fame as a lover was all too well known over the whole of France.

Jean Laval was suspicious and he replied to his Sovereign's invitation that his wife was so shy that she did not wish to appear at Court.

The King was not so easily put off and obstacles only stimulated his interest.

Very shortly a second letter arrived for Jean and he decided to leave for Blois alone.

The King, on his arrival, was extremely disappointed.

"Write to your wife at once," he commanded, "and ask her to leave for Blois immediately."

Jean dutifully wrote a letter which he showed to François.

But he was rubbing his hands gleefully for he had thought up a little strategem.

He had two identical rings made, one of which he left behind with Françoise.

"If I should write and ask you to come to Blois without enclosing the second ring that I am taking with me, answer that you are ill and cannot comply, but if I enclose my ring with the letter, that will signify that it is all right for you to join me."

A few days later, the reply came from Françoise as agreed. She was so sorry, but she was ill.

The King asked Jean to write again, but Jean had committed a great imprudence — he had confided his famous strategem to his Valet.

Hoping for a Royal reward, he revealed it to the King.

One night when the Court was at supper, he stole the ring from Jean's private caskets.

The Royal Goldsmith had the ring copied in record time and restored to its hiding-place.

François, in a gay, malicious mood, kept the Court up late, sang songs of his own composition and organised a competition of gallant tales.

"Ah, how I wish that your beautiful wife were with us, it would do her good, bring her out of her shell, to live at Court for a while. I entreat you, dear Friend, do write to her again — now!"

"Of course, whatever you say, Sire," Jean replied.

"Write your letter tonight and hand it to me in the morning. I shall send it off by special messenger," said the King.

Françoise arrived at Blois in a whirlwind of excitement, and the Courtiers were highly amused by Jean's ill-disguised fury.

As soon as the easily inflammable King looked into Françoise's violet eyes, he fell deeply in love with her.

The lady was not so shy as she had been made out to be, but she was shrewd and had no intention of giving in to the Royal caprice so easily.

It took the King three years to persuade Françoise to share his bed.

This may seem surprising to us in our age of impatient love, but Françoise was a true lover who agreed with Guillaume Lorris that 'who wins the prize must pay the toll, for game hath ever sweeter taste which weary foot hath hotly chased'.

François did not approve of virtuous people. He called

them hypocrites, but it was not his custom to force a woman against her will.

He believed that the greatest pleasure in love is to persuade a woman to capitulate voluntarily.

Jean was eventually sent back to Brittany alone.

His wife did not rejoin him until after François's death in 1547 and all that time he waited to avenge himself on her.

Soon after Françoise arrived home she died in mysterious circumstances.

It was rumoured that she had been murdered by six lackeys at her husband's command and that she had bled to death at his feet.

King Henry II, who now reigned in France, sent a Courtier — Montmorency, to discover the truth, but he reported that he could discover nothing and Jean Laval was acquitted.

Later however, his Will revealed that he had disinherited his nephews and all his other relatives in favour of the Courtier — Montmorency.

KING FRANÇOIS I OF FRANCE

TZAR ALEXANDER II AND PRINCESS KATIA DOLGORUKY.

Tzar Alexander was a handsome, dashing young man who was proud of his excellent horsemanship.

Alexander had various love affairs all his life and was of course, married when he was young.

It should have been a happy marriage, but the Tzarina who was known in Russia as Maria Alexandrovna became tubercular. For many years she lay sick, gradually becoming more querulous and pious and eventually falling entirely under the influence of her Confessor who disapproved of her husband's politics.

It was inevitable that Tzar Alexander and his wife drew apart from each other.

When Alexander was thirty-eight he travelled to Volhynia in order to witness military manoeuvres and he stayed at the Tieplovka Castle which belonged to Prince Mikhail Dolgoruky.

The Dolgorukys were amongst the oldest of Russia's aristocratic families.

Shortly after his arrival Tzar Alexander chanced to see a little girl with long golden hair streaming over her shoulders as she rode her horse hard into a river.

The animal balked and floundered about in a confusion of splashes. The Tzar approached her with some well meaning advice but the child succeeded in getting her horse across the deep water and emerged soaking wet to confront the stranger.

"Who are you?" asked the Tzar.

She told him she was Katherine, Prince Mikhail's daughter.

Katherine was educated at the Smolny Institute in St. Petersburg, an establishment founded by Catherine the Great for young ladies of noble birth.

The Princess was watched by Alexander II. He used to

pay Katherine private visits and whisk her off for rides in his sleigh along the shore of the Gulf of Finland.

Once, huddled with the Tzar under the fur covers, Katherine slipped a pair of scissors out of her muff and cut a little piece out of his coat, which she often wore as a talisman round her neck.

The Tzar arranged that she should be graduated out of Smolny a year earlier than was usual so that after her presentation at Court she could participate in his social life.

He advanced her elder brother Mikhail, in the Army and provided him with the means to marry a beautiful Neapolitan lady.

When their home was established on the road to Peterhof at a convenient distance from the Winter Palace, Katherine went to live with her brother.

Prince Mikhail would come home to find his Sovereign Lord romping on the Dolgoruky floor, up and down the Dolgoruky staircase, with a pile of Dolgoruky dogs and Katherine.

Katherine was an exquisite person. She had a smoothly carved cameo face, with the hint of a smile to make the expression sweet, and impudent Dolgoruky eyes.

Crowning all her enchantment was the dark-gold hair piled up on her small head.

In summertime Tzar Alexander's Court moved to Peterhof, a summer residence Peter the Great had raised to put Versailles to shame, surrounded by immense gardens, stretching to the Bay of Finland.

There in July of 1865 Alexander took Katherine out walking. They came to a small, columned pavilion named Babygone, built on an elevated spot, surrounded by undulating lawns set with flowers and massed with trees.

It was here Katherine became the mistress of Alexander. But before letting her leave him, he showered her with kisses and swore to her:

"Today, Alas, I am not free. But on the first occasion I will marry you, because I consider you my wife before

God. *Au revoir*. I bless you . . .''

Katherine had an old friend, her former Governess, and she said to her:

"How was I able to resist him for a full year? How was it possible I did not love him earlier?"

She was seventeen and the Tzar was forty-five.

In the early years of their love Alexander and Katherine met in a room of the Winter Palace which had once been the office of Nicholas I. Katherine entered it by a side door going onto the street, to which she had a key.

The Tzar came through various corridors, isolated staircases and unused ante-rooms by which the office was separated from the main part of the Palace.

In this room where there were a few portraits some books of military strategy, a scratched desk, and in the corner a couch covered with a rough blue cloth, their love flowered.

Later, news of it filtered through the Court and came to the ears of the Empress, whose illness took a turn for the worse.

The Dolgoruky family found themselves in an unbearable position. Princess Mikhaïl therefore took her young sister-in-law off to Naples to the home of her own family, and there arranged every sort of entertainment for Katherine, balls and parties, picnics and excursions places of ancient legend.

But couriers came daily to Katherine from the Tzar, bringing her letters and Oriental sweets, and romantic mementos of her clandestine life.

When the Tzar went to Paris to attend the Great Exhibition in 1867, Katherine left Naples and joined him in Paris. After an assassination attempt, she rushed to his apartment to make certain of his safety.

He clasped her in his arms and swore that he would never allow himself to be parted from her again.

In 1871 to Katherine's joy and the Tzar's despair she became pregnant. Alexander could not bear the thought that Katherine might die in childbirth, and he dreaded the public revelation of his dishonour.

Katherine hid her condition successfully beneath her heavy winter costume. In May 1872 her pains commenced, and as she had agreed with the Tzar, she went by public coach without a maid to the office of Nicholas I at the Winter Palace.

The Emperor who had received her message joined her at once. Comforted by his presence, her pains grew less, and experienced father as he was, Alexander suggested it was probably a false alarm.

He left her alone to rest on the blue couch, and an old soldier was stationed outside to call him if necessary.

At three o'clock the following morning Veteran woke the Tzar from his bed, and he came to Katherine to find her in immense pain.

A manservant was sent to fetch the doctor and the midwife, but through some misunderstanding neither of them arrived.

For hours Katherine laboured on the blue couch, with the Tzar kneeling beside her, clinging to her hand.

After hours of anguish, the doctor came, but the midwife never did arrive. During the difficult delivery the Tzar of Russia helped the doctor to deliver Katherine's son, while he never ceased to plead:

"Sacrifice the child, but save her at any price!"

The baby was named Yury after Katherine's ancestor who had founded Moscow in 1147.

The first to hear about the birth was the German Ambassador, who had a good spy service. The Imperial Family was outraged. The Empress was said to have received the news in silence and never to have spoken of it.

Shortly afterwards she received from her husband a command to appoint Katherine as Lady-in-Waiting. This meant that the Tzar's mistress would be allowed to move into an apartment in the Winter Palace with her son.

Katherine was installed in a room directly above that

of Alexander which matched his.

In the early seventies the Tzar built his love strongly round Katherine and she had need of a fortress. Her presence in the Palace was a national scandal. Her own family petitioned to deprive her of the right to use their name.

Two years later a daughter was born to Katherine. The Tzar now tackled the matter of the Civil standing of these children. He was obliged to deny them his own name Romanov, so a new surname was devised for Katherine which was Yuryevsky, deprived from her historic ancestry.

The Tzar then issued a secret ukase which raised the children to the dignity of Prince with the title of Highness.

The children lived with Katherine in her apartment above that of the Tzar. An elevator was installed between the two, and Alexander used it every spare moment of the day or night.

He took his State papers to Katherine's room and worked on them from there.

So private was the life of Katherine's apartment that one can only guess the source of the steadfast love between the aging monarch and the young woman.

He romped with his children in that secret apartment, with a pack of dogs playing hide-and-seek amongst the massive gilded furniture.

Letters written by Alexander to Katherine in French and Russian show how happy he was, and what he felt about her:

"Oh, how I love you and the happy times spent with you and our dear children."

"Good morning my soul's angel! I slept well, though sighing not to have you next to me . . ."

"I want to tell you dear, that I love you and my whole life is lived in you. Oh, how I have enjoyed the company of our dear children. God guard these dear beings, and may He give us His blessing one day. I hope you will sleep better than last night, though we won't sleep together —

and we'll both miss that."

The Empress died, and the light coffin of Maria Alexandrovna was borne on the shoulders of her tall sons and the Tzar to the sepulchre of Saints Peter and Paul.

Exactly four weeks later, Alexander told Katherine that on the Sunday when the Fast of St. Peter would end, he would marry her.

One of Alexander's confidants, was brave enough to beg the Tzar to wait for a decent interval.

"I have waited fourteen years," replied the Tzar and he added: "Remember I am master in my own house, and I am the only one who can judge what I have to do."

The marriage took place at Tzarskoe-Selo, the Imperial country seat. The Emperor wore a blue uniform of the Hussars of the Guard and Katherine wore a plain beige dress. He met her before the ceremony, kissed her on the forehead, and said: "Let us go!"

They walked through a long passage to a bare room where the Archpriest, his Assistant and a Psalmist waited for them.

Before a little portable Altar, such as the Army uses, and with the barest of utensils — a Crucifix, a Bible, some candles and the Nuptial Crowns — the Tzar married the woman he had loved since she was ten.

Following instructions, the Archpriest repeated the marriage formula three times with the full title of the groom:

"His Majesty the Emperor Alexander Nikolayevich, the very devoted servant of God, marries Ekaterina Mikhailovna, servant of God."

In recognition of their many kisses the Archpriest gave them no command to kiss each other.

After the ceremony they walked back to a private room, and there Alexander kissed Katherine and in the most ordinary voice invited her to come for a drive.

When they joined his children Alexander said:

"I have waited for this day with fourteen years of

suffering. I cannot go on any longer. I have always had the sensation that a weight would smash my heart.''

His face broke.

''I am afraid for my happiness. Ach! May God not take it away from me too soon!''

Eight months after the wedding on Sunday 13th March 1881 the Tzar's carriage was shattered by terrorists' bombs.

''To the Palace — to die!'' he muttered.

They laid him on the sofa where he had so often kissed Katherine.

When she was fetched the Princess was wearing only a fine negligee. With a heart-rending scream she fell across the body of her husband.

''Sasha! Sasha!'' she cried, but he could not hear her.

His blood soaked her ribbons and laces. In an hour he was dead.

TZAR ALEXANDER II

SHEIKH ABDUL MEDJUEL EL MEZRAB
AND JANE DIGBY (1807-1881)

Sheikh Medjuel El Mezrab followed the personal and nomadic traditions of his people.

He was scholarly, virile and strong with character and a sense of humour.

He was of the desert, but at the same time, he was very different from the majority of Sheikhs and Arabs.

His tribe were a branch of the Anazeh.

They controlled the desert round Palmyra and were, for the tribal habits of their day, a particularly honourable and cultivated lot.

They were neither rich nor numerous, but their blood was blue.

Sheikh Medjuel was the second of nine sons.

His father, the Ruler of the tribe, had been a remarkable man, who had insisted that his children had a wide education.

That Medjuel could read and write was a distinction among the Bedouins. He also spoke several languages.

He had studied the history of ancient Syria.

He knew the desert and the legends of it as very few other Arabs did.

Occasionally he acted as escort for distinguished travellers.

This meant that he earned money for the tribe that was always in need of it and it amused him to have interesting contacts with the outside world.

It was suggested to him that he should act as Guide to an English lady who was very rich and who was coming to Syria.

And so he met the greatest romantic as well as the greatest beauty of her day.

Jane Digby was irresistible, fascinating and reckless.

She had blue eyes which could 'melt a saint'.

Her love affairs, she admitted herself, read like the Almanac de Gotha.

She had married when she was young Lord Ellenborough who was a pompous bore who neglected her.

She became pregnant with Prince Felix Schwarzenberg and bolted with her lover to Paris.

After a short time, she left him and moved to Munich where King Ludwig I, who was a worshipper of beauty became besotted with her and knelt at her feet.

Jane then married Baron Carl-Theodore von Venningen who was young and handsome, but again she found him boring and Count Spyridon Theotky appeared.

The two men fought a duel and Theotky was wounded. Nevertheless he married Jane and the Count was appointed Aide-de-Camp to King Otto of Greece.

It is almost unnecessary to add that he too became Jane's lover, which provoked a wild scandal with recriminations from the Queen.

Because Athens was uncomfortable with such a row going on, Jane went off with a bandit. The Chief of the Pallikares, and she enjoyed the novelty of living in the mountains, until she learnt he was making advances to her lady's-maid.

Jane then decided to go East, where she began an affair with a young Arab called Salih.

It was Salih who suggested she should employ Sheikh Medjuel as her Guide.

To Jane, who had eyes only for Salih, Medjuel was merely a courteous Arab with whom she was negotiating.

The Sheikh, however, was at once intrigued by this unusual and exceedingly beautiful client.

The Arabs watching the preparation which Jane was making to visit the desert called her *'Engleysi'* — a madwoman.

Jane had travelled from England to Europe, from Paris to Greece and all over the Balkans.

Now it was the desert.

She always journied in excessive luxury and she had not learned to live the life of the Bedouins so her enormous caravan was considered by the Arabs to be the idea of a rich maniac.

Among themselves they discussed plans for raiding her.

The expedition started off.

Sheikh Medjuel had brought a large retinue of outriders, horses, bandage covers and foster-camels which he used as travelling dairies.

It mcant mobile milk supplies for the highly bred Arab horses who could obtain no grass in the arid desert wastes.

The camel train moved slowly while Jane and Sheikh Medjuel galloped off into the tawny distance to visit the ruins, encampments or oases which were off their route.

Jane was as tireless a horsewoman in her forties as she had been in her twenties.

She was an Amazon and her whole life was to be spent riding at breakneck speed towards the 'wilder dramas of love'.

She had started life as a daughter of the Earl of Leicester of Holkham, and was born at Holkham Hall, the imposing home of her paternal grandfather, who was the first Earl of Leicester of Holkham.

He was a powerful personality and the greatest landlord and agriculturalist in the County.

Jane had learnt to hunt with fox-hounds.

With Sheikh Medjuel she hunted antelope, wolves and shot partridges.

She also did a little sketching of romantic ruins and what she called 'those poor, dear camels'.

But she was still a tourist 'doing the East' as an outsider.

For Sheikh Medjuel it was love at first sight; a love which bewildered him and gave him a sense of daring.

It was unheard of that he, a Moslem, a Sheikh, should consider *marrying* a Christian.

Yet he knew that if he was to have Jane for himself he must take such a drastic step.

By now he had heard of her affair with Salih and the many others there had been in Europe.

He had no wish to be one of a string of experimental Arab allures.

Jane was, he knew, of social importance, but he did not feel humble in his love for her.

He was an Arab noble, his blood was as blue, if not bluer than hers.

If anything, he wondered whether he himself was not risking making a *mesalliance*.

At night they all sat round the campfire, and flames lit up the faces of the men as they laughed and talked amongst themselves in Arabic.

Jane could not understand. She and the Sheikh spoke a mixture of French and Turkish.

Everything was exciting for Jane as she sat among the Bedouins eating roast lamb basted with sheeps' yoghurt and wild honey.

Outside the circle, the camels barked or groaned in their melancholy way, horses whinnied and far off a jackal howled.

Once again, because Jane always attracted danger, there was a dramatic episode. She had provoked a duel between Venningen and Theotky, but this time the duel was a tribal rather than a personal row, but it was still fought over Jane.

The caravan was on its way about six days out from Damascus when they were suddenly surrounded by a fierce-looking band of horsemen brandishing spears.

The newcomers demanded their money or their lives.

Jane had heard in Damascus many stories of the fate which awaited desert travellers — some never returned.

It was possible that this assault was conducted by Sheikh Medjuel's tribe, but it is more likely he knew nothing about it.

Taken by surprise he was now emotionally involved when he knew he must defend the object of his love.

He rushed to do battle, rallied his own men around him

and, at the point of his lance, routed the marauders, who fled nonplussed.

There was only a few minutes of action, but Jane found the incident extremely stimulating.

Sheikh Medjuel was brave as a lion, a hero, her saviour!.

Back in Damascus, Jane tore herself reluctantly away from the desert, because she had to return to Greece to wind things up in Athens.

She was there in 1853, just long enough to thrill her friends with an account of her latest adventures.

She learned when she arrived back in Syria that her place in Salih's heart had been taken by somebody very young and very beautiful.

Jane found herself shedding tears of regret and having wild longings for the past, and the golden hey-day of her own youth.

Now she was left only with Archaeology.

It was with a mood of black depression that she set out for Baghdad.

She decided there was no going back: England was closed to her, so was Bavaria. So was Paris and Greece.

It was the East that lured her. She loved the land and the life.

When she reached Baghdad she met a man called Sheikh el Barrak, who wished to take her on a journey in to the desert.

It certainly proved a distraction to Jane's melancholy, but once they were out in the wilds, they quarrelled over his unkindness to those 'poor dear camels', and the fact that he invited several strangers into her private tent.

It is however not easy to rid one's-self of a caravan *en route* and when they reached Aleppo they were on very bad terms, but they continued their journey together.

It was then Jane found herself thinking affectionately of Sheikh Medjuel, who was a different type of El Barrak and, in her own words, 'a gentleman'.

News of her arrival in Damascus soon reached Medjuel

in the desert.

When he heard she was riding towards Damascus accompanied by the Sheikh El Barrak he acted swiftly.

Suddenly he rode out of the distant sky to meet her bringing her a beautiful Arab mare as a present.

Sheikh Barrak disappeared and together Jane and Sheikh Medjuel returned to the City.

Jane discovered in him all the qualities and attractions she had so often imagined she had found in other men, only to be disappointed.

This time she was not deceived, for Sheikh Medjuel had character, brains and breeding and he loved her for herself.

This was proved during the thirty years of their life together, when he was never the least interested in her fortune.

A man of honour and kindness, he was also, Jane discovered, a man of romantic passion.

During her absence, he had divorced his wife who had borne him sons and was, by Arab standards, an old woman.

She was given the dowry she had originally brought and honourably pensioned off.

Sheikh Medjuel was therefore free to marry Jane.

He proposed to her as they rode towards Palmyra. Jane accepted in a mood of rapture and excitement, and received his first kiss.

Now there would be no more disenchantment for her. She had found the perfect man and the perfect life.

The English Consul was horrified at the idea of her marriage and even went so far as to question her sanity, but it was not within his power to prevent it.

Jane had made up her mind. Official barriers were swept aside and the marriage took place at Homs, where Medjuel owned a house, although he always preferred living in his tents in the desert.

Surprisingly, Jane was loved and accepted by the Mezrab tribe. She was known as their *Sitt,* or lady; or more picturesquely, *Umn-el-Laban,* Mother of Milk, in reference to her fair skin.

She was ecstatically happy amongst them — she felt she had come home.

Jane was quick to adapt to Arab ways.

She smoked the *Narghilye,* and liked to go barefooted, wearing the traditional blue robe and *yashmak.*

She learned to outline her eyes with the smudge of kohl, that is an essential part of an Arab woman's make-up.

Her splendid horsemanship and her love of horses, as well as her knowledge of them which she had learned at the Holkham stables, was appreciated by the Arabs.

Jane and Medjuel hunted.

There were falcons, Persian hounds, and soon she had mastered the art of dromedary-riding.

She was content and almost supremely happy.

She loved Medjuel over-whelmingly and because of it there was always sadness when Medjuel went off alone into the desert for two-months' sheep-herding expedition, in order to earn money for his tribe.

It never occurred to him to avail himself of her fortune as so many other men had done.

She learned now that the dull Lord Ellenborough, her first husband, had also reached the East.

He had become Governor-General of India.

Had she remained as his wife she would have found these gold-fringed pavilions stifling.

A thousand times better, she thought, were the black Bedouin tents of her Mezrabi.

She had learned to speak Arabic fluently, but everybody agreed that Medjuel spoke the most classical Arabic in the whole of Syria.

Medjuel and Jane, however, both had too strong a personality to live a serene idyll.

There were lovers' quarrels, reconciliations, jealousies, and always the emotional passions, which even time could not quench.

There were romantic honeymoon journeys alone together in the desert, with misunderstandings, quarrels and partings.

On Jane's side there was the gnawing agony of jealousy. But whatever happened, life was never dull.

What was so extraordinary was that at fifty, Jane looked as though she was still in her thirties and she kept her figure.

Eleven years later the famous Abd El Kadir wrote:

"She was the most beautiful woman. At the time I write she is sixty-one, tall, commanding and Queen-like. She was grande dame au bout desdoigts, as much as if she had just left the Salons of London and Paris, refined in manner and voice, nor did she ever utter a word you could wish unsaid.

Mrs. Richard Burton gushed:

"She was the honoured and respected Queen of her tribe, wearing one blue garment, her beautiful hair in two long plaits down to the ground, milking the camels, serving her husband, preparing his food, giving him water to wash his hands and face, sitting on the floor washing his feet, giving him his coffee, his sherbet, and while he ate she stood and waited on him, and gloried in it."

The truth was that Jane never grew old.

At sixty-two years of age she was still the romantic girl of seventeen with ardent, passionate feelings.

What was more, she looked young, she felt young and she remained romantically and passionately in love with Medjuel and he loved her deeply in return.

There were no flaunted mistresses, nor did he ever wish for another wife.

When she was seventy-four Jane found the long desert rides becoming too exhausting for her.

For some months before her death she had to remain in Damascus, while her horses grew restless in the stables.

Medjuel went to and from the desert without her and she felt it bitterly.

Because she was a realist, she bought her grave in the

Protestant cemetery.

Then during the Summer of 1881, cholera swept through the city.

Most of the Europeans left for the hills.

Jane and Medjuel stayed on in the beautiful house, with its fountains, its gardens, and the menagerie.

The end came quickly on August 11th, and Medjuel was with his beloved wife when she died.

It had been for nearly thirty years an adventure of romance and beauty of the East, which was the revelation of her life.

With him, as Sir Richard Burton wrote: 'life's poetry never sank to prose.'

After her death, as in her life, there was drama.

As the funeral cortege moved slowly towards the Protestant cemetery, Medjuel's heart rebelled.

He hurled himself out of the first carriage and took to his heels like a madman.

The cortege went on its way and the Service was conducted to its close.

Suddenly there was the sound of horse's hooves thundering nearer.

On Jane's favourite black mare he galloped up to the open grave.

Jane's Bedouin husband and her Arab horse were there beside her at the very last.

SHEIKH ABDUL MEZRAB

H.S.H. PRINCE HONORÉ III OF MONACO

1731-1795

Honoré III of Monaco, unlike his predecessors was determined to marry for love.

He was also in no hurry.

He was at Versailles in 1750 when he met the *Marquise* de Brignole-Sale.

She came from a great Genoese family, the Balbis.

She was very good-looking and intelligent but she had a haughty manner and a hasty temper.

Her marriage had not been a great success.

The *Marquis* de Brignole-Sale was enormously wealthy and he was descended from a line of Doges.

Although he was kind-hearted he was somewhat slow-witted and obstinate.

He was irritated by his wife's whims and fancies, so he gave way to her with a surly resignation.

The *Marquis* and *Marquise* had one child, a daughter.

Marie-Catherine was eleven years old.

The *Marquise* went to Paris and received a flattering welcome.

Her educated brain made her acceptable in the Salons of the most intelligent and cultured Society of the period.

Passions at that age came to the fore in society.

When a woman fell in love with someone younger than herself, she did so deeply and passionately.

It was love at first sight when she met Honoré Grimaldi.

There was something sharp and sensual about him which attracted an experienced and intelligent woman like the *Marquise*.

Honoré had a troubled boyhood and his imprisonment during the battle of his nation had given him an uneasy mind and a heart more inclined to be suspicious than affectionate.

He was however the kind of man that all women find

attractive.

Honoré and the *Marquise* arranged matters tactfully and discreetly so that there was no scandal.

There was an uncommon understanding between them.

She gave way to the greater love while he let himself be loved, partly because he was only thirty, while she was forty.

In 1754 Honoré III went to Monaco and also spent several months in Genoa, staying at the Palazzo Rosso.

The *Marquis* had no liking for him. His elegance irritated him and he considered his courteous indifference to be just sly hypocrisy.

Honoré did not upset himself because of his host's animosity.

He had discovered that as well as the *Marquise*, there was a daughter of nearly fifteen.

Marie-Catherine was tall, slender, well-developed and graceful in her movements.

She had blonde hair, dark blue eyes and a fresh complexion.

She was, according to a critic of the day, 'as lovely as an angel'.

For the past fifteen years, Honoré had rejected all idea of marriage, but when he returned to France he was turning it over in his mind.

On the death of his father in 1751, Honoré became the fifth Duke of Valentinois and his official Reception took place on March 17th 1755.

He had become aware of the urgency to ensure the continuance of his line.

His brother, the Count de Valentinois had no children after more than five years of marriage.

The *Marquise* de Brignole spent the Winter and Summer of that year in France and brought her daughter with her.

She must have been aware of what was happening between Marie-Catherine and the Prince of Monaco.

Honoré III had made her sign a written promise of

marriage which read:

"I, the undersigned, declare and promise to the Prince of Monaco never to marry anyone but him, whatever may happen, and never to listen to any proposal that might tend to release me."

The consent of the *Marquis* still had to be obtained, but Marie-Catherine did not dare face her father herself, but left it to her mother.

The sweeping demands and outbursts of the *Marquise* annoyed him so much that they merely made him firmer in his refusal.

Weeks, then months went by, but he did not seem to alter and Honoré became discouraged.

He started discussions with the Duke de La Valliere for the hand of his daughter.

The Duke thought there would be no difficulty in persuading Louis XV to grant permission, seeing the honours that had been held by the Grimaldis.

Honoré wrote to the *Marquise* at Genoa on May 3rd telling her of these negotiations.

A month later, he received a reply which contained no reproach, but merely the hope that Honoré was making a choice that would be a happy one for him.

It was not without regret that he turned away from a Genoese alliance.

He still thought that Marie-Catherine's sweet nature seemed an assurance of happiness and her family fortune an assurance of power.

He let another month go by before taking up the matter with the Duke de La Valliere any further.

Then early in July the Duke placed the application before the King.

However, as soon as the news broke there was a cry of protest from the Dukes and Peers.

Honoré nevertheless made quite certain that everything would end well and he returned the written promise of marriage to the *Marquise* de Brignole.

The envelope contained the words:

"This belongs to Madame Anne Balbi de Brignole, of Genoa, and must only be given into her hands, or against an order signed by her. At Paris, this 19th of July."

Honoré then wrote a letter to the King, hoping to force the Royal hand, but it apparently had no effect because he was informed that the support of the Ministers was insufficient to allow the Marriage Contract to go through.

The following day the marriage negotiations were broken off.

It was a great disappointment for Honoré III and to make matters worse, a wrathful letter arrived from the *Marquise*.

She was one of those tempestuous people who do not believe in half measures.

A triumphant Honoré greatly annoyed her; an Honoré defeated by a clique aroused her sympathy.

He had left Versailles for Monaco.

The *Marquise* wanted him to have a striking revenge which would enable him to return to Court in triumph.

Marie-Catherine did not know what had been happening.

But she was aware that her mother was making further attempts and fresh energy to get her father to consent to the marriage.

The *Marquis* sulked and kept to his own rooms.

Honoré III, aware of his prospective father-in-law's hostility became very exacting over the terms of the Marriage Contract.

By the end of October 1756, matters had reached a stage where the *Marquise* just managed to prevent her husband from publishing a decree which would have forbidden the Brignole heiress to transfer her wealth outside the Genoese Republic.

Then, unexpectedly, the *Marquis* and his daughter had a talk together; just the two of them, that lasted for a couple of hours.

He said he was worried over the difference in their ages

— Honoré was nineteen years older than Marie-Catherine and he feared the Prince had a difficult character.

He asked his daughter to confide in him and tell him her 'intimate thoughts'; if she really wanted to marry the Prince.

He promised that if so, he would overcome his dislike.

Marie-Catherine could only talk of her love and the *Marquis* gave his consent.

A week later, Marie-Catherine wrote to Honoré saying: *"I deserve no praise for obeying Papa, for the consent he has just given you in no way preceded mine."*

At last, by June all the difficulties were smoothed over, the contract signed, jewels were sent to Marie-Catherine which were acknowledged to be 'most admirable and of perfect splendour'.

The seventeen-year-old Marie-Catherine wrote to her *fiance*:

"It is a flattering to me as it is pleasant, Monsieur, that you should feel as I do about this conclusion on which my whole happiness depends; it will be perfect if I can indeed hope that yours does too. Please believe that I will do all I can to contribute to that. Although Mama must have sent you my thanks for your beautiful presents, I cannot allow myself not to repeat them . . ."

The wedding took place by proxy in Genoa, on June 15th 1757.

The young bride went aboard a splendidly decorated galley, accompanied by her mother and relatives and a large retinue.

Ships of the Republic escorted it ceremoniously as far as the territorial waters of Monaco.

It was then that the whole arrangement practically broke down.

The *Marquise* de Brignole-Sale, highly conscious of her birth and rank, maintained that the Prince should come out to greet his wife on the galley.

But Honoré, a Sovereign Prince, refused to 'go any

farther than the landing-stage'.

The *Marquise* was indignant, negotiations began and continued for days.

The account of this episode is contained in a letter written by one of Honoré's household to a friend, several days later.

"You will remember that when you left Monaco, the Genoese boat had dropped back to outside our waters, taking the precious charge, the object of our regrets, with it. These proud Republicans still persisted in wanting the Prince to go to collect his Princess from their boat; and the Prince remained unshakeable in his determination to do nothing of the kind. After six days of useless negotiations, of letters and messengers being sent back and forth, the famous Colonel Millo was deputized to come to an arrangement over the final expedient proposed by the Genoese.

This was to make a bridge out from the Condamine landing-stage to join one let down from their boat. The next day, Colonel Millo's Embassy, having settled the matter, a general post sounded and we all took our positions for the great event. The Fleet arrived in the harbour, the Palace guns fired a salute, the Prince and his Court came down to the shore, the galley drew near our bridge and started to lower another, as had been agreed. When the Prince grew tired of waiting for the end of what seemed a long job, and became impatient to embrace his darling bride he jumped into a boat followed by his intrepid Courtier and in spite of the fuss reached the galley's ladder. He had scarcely put foot on it when the Princess came down followed by her mother, three uncles and a cousin. The flags and banners were hoisted, the galley-slaves saluted the guns thundered, and the people shouted with joy.

They are now at the Prince's summer-house at Carnoles, where we find the peace of the countryside a relief after the tumult of the capital . . ."

There was no doubt of Marie-Catherine's tender love for her husband.

She wrote to him in the Summer of 1760, when he had to journey to Paris, the following letter:

"My dear love, I swear I feel as deeply as you how cruel it is to be separated from the one you love most in the whole world, and although I am very happy to be with my parents, who are most kind to me, my sorrow at your absence is ever with me. I am only truly happy when dreaming, for then I have always the feeling of being with you . . .and I am always happy to see that you respond affectionately to the signs I give of my tenderness for you; but waking up is cruel, for however much I look, I do not find you . . ."

H.S.H. PRINCE HONORÉ III OF MONACO AND
CATHERINE DE BRIGNOLE

TSAR ALEXANDER I AND JULIE DE KRUDENER

When Julie de Krudener lost her husband, she was thirty-eight, but still beautiful, a graceful woman with a musical voice and a smile of pure radiance.

She reproached herself bitterly on the death of the Baron who had been older than her by twenty years.

She realised she should have made more fuss of him and granted him the company of his children.

To make amends, she settled in Lyons and wrote a novel about a young Countess whose husband was twenty years older than herself.

But in the face of all temptation she remained faithful to him from beginning to end.

During the Battle of Waterloo Tsar Alexander went to Heilbronn, which was the headquarters of the Russian Army.

His first action was to open the Holy Book which he always had with him, but his mind could not grasp the sense of what he was reading.

He had written a letter to Countess Edling about his problem and she had told him about a *Madame* de Krudener who was deeply religious.

The Tsar was sitting in his bedroom thinking of the Countess who had told him about the lady called *Madame* de Krudener.

The Tsar said he would like to make her acquaintance.

"But how am I ever to meet her?" the Tsar asked himself.

The thought had barely flashed through his mind when there was a knock on the door.

It was Prince Polotsky to say that he was sorry to trouble him, but he could not get rid of a lady who had insisted on seeing him.

Her name was *Madame* de Krudener.

The Tsar was astonished. He seemed to be in a dream.

"*Madame* de Krudener! *Madame* de Krudener!" he exclaimed.

Such a quick response to his desire could not be mere chance. He received her immediately.

Julie de Krudener did not waste a moment in offering civilities to the Tsar.

She confronted him at once with reproof of his various sins of pride and the immorality of his life.

Her idea of their correction was to throw himself with her at the foot of the cross.

The Tsar listened with his head in his hands, shedding tears.

Then Julie suddenly recollected that she was speaking to her Sovereign and begged his forgiveness.

"Do not be afraid," he replied. "Your whole speech is justified in my heart."

They embraced like children, ecstatic with shared smiles and tears.

They confessed their sins to one another and forgave them. They prayed and they were cleansed.

The Tsar commanded Julie to follow him to Heidelburg. She came with her little band of disciples and took up residence in the crude ante-room of a cattle-shed.

"I also have my guard," she told the Emperor coquettishly pointing to a couple of cows.

In this humble place the Tsar spent his nights with Julie praying. He told her that for years he daily read three chapters of The Bible, one from the Old Testament, one from The Gospels and one from The Epistles.

But he had not succeeded in uprooting from his soul one solitary sin.

The news of the final defeat at the Battle of Waterloo came to the Tsar and he set out for Paris.

At Julie's behest he gave out quantities of money to the poor along the way.

She followed with her party and after a distressful journey they reached Paris and were installed at the request of the Tsar at the Hotel de Montchenu.

A garden door opened onto the Champs Élysées as did that of the Élysée Palace which the Tsar had prepared for himself.

Julie had left Paris as a successful novelist.

She returned now as a prophetess and a Saint with the Tsar under her thumb.

Everybody was astonished.

Her Salon, which consisted of very few rooms offered guests rush-bottom chairs, sermons and prayer groups.

For persons with spiritual problems a private audience might be had with *Madame* de Krudener in a small back room.

Dull though it sounds, it was still the most fashionable Salon in Paris.

There came *Madame* Chateaubriand, Benjamin Constant, *Madame* de Stael, Madame Recamier, and all the significant Dukes and Duchesses.

They all went to wonder at the sight of Julie.

Clothed in white, she first prostrated herself then gracefully rose and with her thin hair, her inspired manner and her high voice, seemed to enjoy the astonishment that came over the faces of the visitors.

Some said they liked it and some said they did not.

Every alternative evening, and far into the night, the Tsar spent with Julie, submitting his short-comings to her prayer for correction, with such good results that she was able to write to *Mademoiselle* Stourdza;

"His attitude has been that of a Christian hero, such as with the help of Almighty I hardly dared to predict last year."

However Alexander's Christian heroism was not always beyond reproach.

Julie was also to write unhappily about being invited to suffer "the humiliation of an earthly relationship."

Even at fifty she retained the elegant and elastic movements of a natural dancer.

Her voice was described as 'melodious, flexible and gentle'.

Her conversational powers were 'fluent to an alarming degree'.

But she was a mere wisp of the curvaceous blonde whose portrait had been painted by Angelica Kauffman.

In the reign of the last Tsar, a Royal Historian was permitted to examine the Imperial archives.

He found evidence that large bags of gold were transferred from Alexander's privy purse to Baroness de Krudener.

He also found many dressmakers' bills.

But the outcome of this extraordinary friendship was the Treaty of the Holy Alliance which Alexander asked the states of Europe to sign.

The British however, did not sign.

They expressed regret that British Constitutional practice made participation impossible.

TZAR ALEXANDER I

KING LEOPOLD OF THE BELGIANS

KING LEOPOLD OF THE BELGIANS
SOVEREIGN OF THE CONGO FREE STATES
AND CAROLINE DELACROIX

1835-1909

Caroline Delacroix was the daughter of a poverty-stricken railway mechanic and the youngest of his thirteen children.

Caroline was sent to work in a Laundry while another sister sold vegetables from a hand-barrow at Les Halles in Paris.

In order to escape the drudgery of the Laundry, Caroline became the mistress of a cocky gambler who frequented the Race-Tracks.

He was out doing his usual ploys when Caroline's doorbell rang and a strange woman told her she had been observed in the Champs Élysées Palace Hotel by a very distinguished personage.

She told Caroline to go to a certain address the following day, where she would find something to her advantage.

Curious, Caroline went to the agreed address, and as she was shown into a Sitting-Room, she heard a man of Military bearing say to someone in a chair:

"Yes, Sire, yes, Sire."

Caroline was cute enough to know that she was in the presence of Royalty.

She sank to her knees before the man in the chair.

He held out his hands and she kissed them.

The man was Leopold, King of the Belgians.

Caroline's life changed over night.

She travelled with the King everywhere, took the same train, alighted at the same destination, stayed at the same Hotel and ate at the same Dining-Room.

Yet she was forbidden to speak to him in public, or acknowledge his presence in any way.

Every morning she was under instructions to walk in the Park with her maid, where King Leopold would meet her.

With an air of amazement he would bid her a loud "Good-morning!"

The maid would then fall back with the King's *Aide-de-Camp*, while Leopold walked next to *Tres Belle*, as he called Caroline.

On rainy days the same performance took place between carriages.

In 1902 the Queen died and the King no longer played games.

He was a King and he considered that hypocricy was beneath his dignity.

If the Belgians did not approve of his mistress, there was nothing they could do.

The people of Belgium were infuriated at the sight of the favourite, especially at the time when the Congo scandals broke all over the world.

Magazines were then filled with photographs of Negroes without hands, the Cannibal Coburg feasting upon the bodies of natives.

Decent people holding their noses in the presence of the Belgian crown.

When Caroline went shopping in Brussels, she was insulted.

One day housewives gathered to throw stones at her.

After this incident, the King called the Minister of the Interior and informed him that if Caroline was obliged to leave Belgium on account of such behaviour, he, their King would leave also.

He would abdicate.

Caroline, however had deadlier enemies than the mob.

The Princesses Louise, Stephanie and Clementine were determined to rid their father of Caroline, and to prevent him from visiting *Tres Belle*.

Now on informal occasions Caroline was the King's hostess when he summoned to his table the most exciting and significant people in Europe.

She accompanied the King on a Mediterranean cruise during which she was officially received everywhere.

On this journey *Tres Belle* became pregnant.

Their son was born after a long and painful labour during which the King did not leave her side for an instant.

He awarded her with the Honorary title; Baroness de Vaughan.

The Princesses were now in a panic.

Tres Belle had to be seduced away from the King.

Handsome, gallant young Courtiers were introduced to her company.

Fortunately for Caroline, her servants were excellent friends with the Princess Clementine's servants, so she had a spy who told her what was being plotted against her.

Eleven months after her first child, *Tres Belle* became pregnant again, and the attacks against her increased in virulence.

Her enemies now determined that the King must be persuaded to believe that the new child was not his own.

In order to remove the woman he loved to a friendlier climate, the King rented for her the Château de Lormois near Paris where he visited her faithfully three times a week.

She was happy there and had friends around her.

For once the gossips had something really to talk about.

The child who came into the world on Leopold's Saint's Day was born without a hand.

The King listened behind the door while the Doctor broke the news to Caroline.

Then he came in, shaking with sobs and gathered her into his arms.

As Leopold grew older he became lame, but his brain remained as lucid and incisive as it ever was.

He devoted his last years to securing his vast fortune against the depredation of the Princesses.

He arranged for the transfer of his beautifully tended estates and great parklands to the people he loved on his death.

One year before he died he turned over the Congo Free State to the Belgian Government.

He continued to love *Tres Belle*, he delighted in his sons.

He would go into public markets, fill his pockets with sweets and load his pockets down with toys and treasure-laden returned to them.

He appointed a Lawyer to find a way by which they could legally be recognised and entitled Princes of Coburg.

It was then that Princess Clementine made another attempt at trying to separate her father from 'that noxious woman'.

She consulted Cardinal Mercier, Primate of Belgium, and the Cardinal agreed to carry the matter to The Pope.

When he returned, the Cardinal requested the King to come to Brussels for a Conference.

The King went and was away for a week during which time Caroline was tense with anxiety.

The following morning, after his return, the King entered her room and asked:

"Do you know what the Holy Father said to His Eminence?"

Tres Belle shook her head.

"The Sovereign Pontiff decided that I would either have to send you away, or marry you. I assured the Cardinal that I would obey the Holy Father and marry you."

Caroline nearly fainted with relief.

He then returned to Brussels to arrange everything.

A week went by, then *Tres Belle* received a telegram: "COME AT ONCE."

She went to join Leopold at Laeken where she found him in a very loving and attentive mood.

But afterwards he took her hand and said:

"You will have to be very brave, *Tres Belle*. You have to be, for I am going to die!"

The Doctors had discovered that he had an intestinal complaint and had been in conference for the past week.

He was to be operated on within the next two days.

Because he was already seventy-four years old, his chances were slim.

At nine o'clock the next morning, *Tres Belle* made confession and took Communion.

She then joined the King who was wearing a white flannel dressing-gown, while she wore a black gown.

The Canon of Laeken Castle was also there to marry them.

The King then called one of his trusted Ministers and said:

"I present you with my widow. I place her under your protection."

The marriage papers were reposed with the Church.

Later, with a shaking hand the King signed the decree which would in 1914 enable the Belgians to hold a narrrow bridge of war.

This would perhaps spare Western Europe from the possibility of being ruled by the Kaiser.

Then he whispered:

"The King is content."

Before the King died he had made his beloved *Tres Belle* the Baroness de Vaughan, and she now left Belgium.

Her love for the King had been long and faithful, which might to the Belgians have seemed strange in view of the fact that their King had chosen a girl from the streets.

But their hearts had beaten together and she had given him an unbelievable happiness, which few Kings are lucky enough to know.

*H.R.H. PRINCE FREDERICK PRINCE OF WALES
AND ANNE VANE*

H.R.H. PRINCE FREDERICK LEWIS
AND ANNE VANE

Heir Apparent of H.M. King George II of England and Elector of Hanover, the 15th Prince of Wales Frederick Lewis had suffered through an unhappy childhood.

Born in Hanover on January 6th 1707 he was left behind alone in Hanover when his parents accompanied his Grandfather, H.M. King George I to claim the British throne in London.

He was permitted to run wild with all manner of rough children. He enjoyed the company of roistering musicians and his education suffered dramatically. No Tutor could control this wild colt-like youth.

He spent much of his time in low company in the Taverns. He had an amorous sexual liaison with Madame D'Elitz, who had previously slept with his father and even his grandfather.

By the time he was finally summoned to London by his family, he had already had a frustrated elopement. His Grandfather, H.M. King George I had arranged his engagement to another grandchild, Wilhelmina of Prussia.

Because the future George II absolutely hated his own father, this arrangement was terminated officially as soon as George II succeeded to the thrones of Britain and Hanover.

Strong-willed Frederick Lewis disobeyed his father's command, and disregarding the break-off of his engagement, he attempted to run away with her.

However Wilhelmina's mother, George II's sister, heard of the plot and told The King, who then had Frederick Lewis stopped on his way, once and for all.

Frederick Lewis was left in London to mingle with the same type of low-life musicians and tavern louts he had known in Hanover. He had a succession of debauched affairs. Then he met Mary Vane.

She really loved Frederick Lewis, and said: "I would have died for him!"

They had a son together and Mary Vane claimed that Frederick Lewis had married her in secret. Later that claim was legally disproved.

Frederick Lewis after several years was no longer in love with Mary Vane.

He left her to pursue the granddaughter of the first Duke and Duchess of Marlborough, Lady Diana Spencer.

The Duchess of Marlborough however, the former close friend and confidante of the late Queen Anne, offered a huge dowry of £100,000 to consolidate the affair.

She wanted her granddaughter to be The Queen of England, but the bait of £100,000 was deemed insuffficient by King George II, who so hated his eldest son that he was determined that he should not marry for love.

George II next suggested to the Danes that his eldest son Frederick Lewis should claim as his bride the deformed and mentally-retarded Princess of Denmark, Aurelia.

When Frederick Lewis was absolutely appalled and refused to wed Aurelia, a compromise was reached by father and son.

In spite of their constant bickering, they settled on Augusta of Saxe-Gotha. She was seventeen, timid, and so childish that she arrived at the Court carrying a huge doll.

If Mary Vane had found something to love in Frederick Lewis so had Augusta. She produced eight children for Frederick during his lifetime and was pregnant at the time of his untimely death.

Frederick Lewis caught a cold from sweltering in Parliament, then returned to Kew from Westminster in an open carriage. A canker he had received from playing cricket burst, and he was dead within a few hours, in March 1751.

Augusta was miserably unhappy but Frederick Lewis's father George II who happened to be playing cards when the news was brought to his attention, so hated him that on the day of his death, he remarked casually about it and played the next card without pausing.

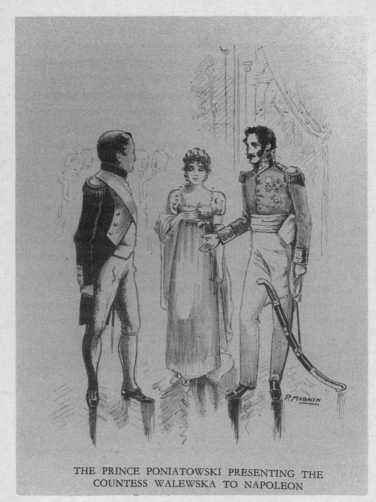

THE PRINCE PONIATOWSKI PRESENTING THE
COUNTESS WALEWSKA TO NAPOLEON

*EMPEROR NAPOLEON I AND
MADAME WALEWSKA*

EMPEROR NAPOLEON AND MARIE WALEWSKA

Napoleon stopped to change horses on his way to Warsaw at a Posting Station in the little town of Blonie.

His carriage was immediately surrounded by an excited crowd.

Two young women managed to force their way through the cheering peasants.

The prettiest of them, a blonde with melting deep blue eyes and wearing a national head-dress, said to Duroc, the Grand Marshal, in French:

"Please, please, *Monsieur,* take us to the Emperor and give me a chance to speak to him, if only for a moment."

The Grand Marshal took a long look at the pretty Pole and decided that his master would be only too glad to make her acquaintance.

"Come along," he said, taking the young woman's arm and led her to the door of the Imperial carriage.

"Sire, here is a young lady who has braved all the dangers of this mob for your sake," he said. "She insists upon speaking to you."

Napoleon looked at the pretty girl and was delighted.

He took off his hat and leaned out to speak to her.

Blushing furiously, but carried away by her feelings, the little Pole seized his hand and kissed it.

"Welcome, welcome to our country!" she cried. "Nothing we can do to express our feelings towards you or our happiness on seeing you tread the soil of a land which is only waiting for your presence to rise as one man!"

The Emperor was touched and picking up a bouquet he had been given, offered it to the young woman.

"Keep it," he said, "as a pledge of my good intentions. We shall meet again in Warsaw, I hope, and I shall insist on a thank you from your own pretty mouth."

He then recalled his Grand Marshal and gave the order to proceed. The carriage soon disappeared.

The crowd cheering excitedly saw Napoleon waving his hat to an unknown blonde.

Her name was Marie Walewska.

Daughter of an old, but very poor Polish family, she was an emotional little girl, more interested in the fate of her country than dressing her dolls.

When she was seventeen her mother insisted that she marry the Count Anastase Colonna de Walewice-Walewski, a rich land-owner of sixty and when Marie protested, beat her into submission.

She was led to the altar. But she continued to live in hope that the French Emperor, whom she idolised, would come one day to deliver her country.

Napoleon had hardly set foot in the Palace in Warsaw than he began to talk of the little blonde at Blonie.

"You must find me that young woman," he said to the Grand Marshal. "I do not mind how − but I want to see her again!"

When he learned that his young admirer was married to an old man, Napoleon rubbed his hands together and sent the Grand Marshal to Prince Poniatovski, War Minister in the Provisional Government.

"Tell him," Napoleon said, "that I am interested in this young lady, and wish to meet her again as soon as possible."

The Grand Marshal gave the message to the Prince who planned to turn Napoleon's interest in Marie to political account.

"Be good enough to inform His Majesty that I will arrange a Ball for him tomorrow evening, where he will meet this young woman again."

While the Grand Marshal went off to give the Emperor the good news, Marie received the Prince and was startled when he said:

"I know that you met Napoleon in Blonie. Now all this all-powerful Monarch wants is to see you again. The interest he shows in you is an unlooked-for chance for our country.''

Facing the Prince with his knowing smile, Marie was dumbfounded. She thought the purpose of her action was being mistaken and tears came into her eyes.

"No," she said, "I will not go!"

"I repeat," the Prince frowned, "that Providence may be able to use you to restore our dear Poland."

Marie did not yield, and was still resisting when her husband came in.

He was immensely proud that his wife had been invited to the Ball.

There was nothing she could do but accept.

When the Emperor arrived at the Ball he caught sight of Marie and called the Prince who immediately said:

"A certain person has been impatiently waiting for you. He has ordered that you should join in the dance."

"I do not dance," Marie replied, "and I do not want to dance!"

But at last Napoleon and Marie met. She felt embarrassed and forgot to curtsy.

"I am sure you have something to say to me," Napoleon said:

The way he spoke restored her confidence.

She replied that like all her countrymen she had only one wish and that was to see Poland restored by him within her ancient frontiers.

"That is a tall order," Napoleon smiled, "you must help me bring it about."

A few minutes later he left the Ballroom.

Marie had hardly arrived home when her maid handed her a note which read:

"You are the only one I saw; you alone I admired; you alone I want. A quick reply to calm the impatient longing of

N"

Marie saw only the words: *"You alone I want."*

She crumpled up the note and told the Prince who was

waiting in the street there was no answer.

The Prince begged Marie through the bedroom door to yield to the Emperor's wishes.

For half-an-hour the War Minister tried to make Marie see the beauty and purity of the sacrifice demanded of her, but he left without an answer.

When she awoke the next morning there was another note.

When Marie was dressed a Government delegation accompanied by Grand Marshal Duroc, was announced.

On her husband's orders, although she said she had a headache, she was forced to receive the visitors.

The delegation told her to attend a dinner that evening then departed. Marie, urged by her husband, called on *Madame* du Vaubin, who was Prince Poniatovski's mistress, and asked her advice.

Madame de Vauban was in the plot. She read her an amazing letter, which finished:

"Men at the head of public affairs cannot get anything good done by their decisions unless they enlist the help of women."

Marie was shaken by this and Madame de Vauban handed her Napoleon's second note, the one she had refused to open. She read:

". . . you give me no rest. Please bring a little gaiety and happiness to a heart which is only too ready to worship you. It is hard to get one answer. You owe me two.
N."

Marie finally agreed and was taken to Zamek where a reception attended by Napoleon was to be held.

When he reached Marie he merely bowed and after dinner, returned to his apartments. The Grand Marshal and members of the Government immediately surrounded Marie.

"Wonderful!" they said. "He had eyes only for you! He was burning for you! Only you can sway his heart and get him to restore Poland!"

At that moment the Grand Marshal gave Marie a letter.

The guests cheered, but Marie burst into tears. Napoleon had written:

"You alone can remove the obstacles between us . . . Come! Please come! All your wishes will be met. Your country will be dearer to me when you have taken pity on a poor heart.

N."

Amazed at such brashness, Marie could not even look up. She could only whisper:

"Do what you will with me."

The patriots fell on each other's necks.

She arranged to visit the Emperor that night between ten and eleven. She arrived pale and silent.

She was taken up to the Emperor's room, but while he talked to her she wept and sobbed so much that the Emperor failed to get any response and she remained unsullied.

The next morning she was sent a casket containing a diamond nosegay and tiara which she threw furiously on the floor.

But after dinner, under pressure of the patriots she was taken back to the Emperor.

They talked for a little until with an angry gesture Napoleon pulled out his fob watch.

"Look," he said, throwing it down and stamping on it. "that is what I will do to Poland if you refuse me."

"His eyes flashed right through me," Marie wrote long afterwards. *"I seemed to be having a horrible nightmare. All I wanted was to wake up, but his savage stare seemed to fire darts which nailed me to my seat . . .*

"I was trembling. I heard sound — the noise made by his heels stamping on the poor watch.

"Suddenly I had a feeling of relief. Was I awake at last? I thought. But what happened? A weight descended upon me and I gasped for air . . ."

Marie had fainted and Napoleon's moment had come.

When she came to Marie was horrified to realise that Napoleon had had his will of her.

The Emperor, sprawling in a wing chair near the fire was slowly getting his breath back.

Marie reflected that she must profit by the situation in the interests of her country. Protests, hard words or hysterics could not undo what had just been done.

Quite the opposite — the Emperor might lose his temper, go back on his promises and have her thrown out for good.

She rose, walked up to him and tried to smile.

Napoleon looked a little uneasy, but she fell on her knees and said:

"I forgive you."

The words were a relief. He seized her hands, kissed them and swore they would see a lot more of each other in the future.

She looked at him very seriously and asked:

"Do you really believe I could go home now and resume my life with my husband? Never! What has happened makes you and me one, and prevents me from returning to the man I married."

Napoleon was extremely embarrassed, but Marie now seemed deeply concerned to continue the liaison and pressed her warm lips on the palm of his hand. The contact made him quiver.

The Imperial passion, assuaged for a moment, revived.

"You are right!" Napoleon said. "Will you come to live with me?"

Then he picked her up, carried her to the sofa and amid a whirl of petticoats demonstrated what he had done while she was in a faint.

Marie was duly installed in the Palace and her liaison with the Emperor became official.

She had a special position as her country's Ambassador to the Emperor, *his Polish wife*.

One night when Napoleon was being enterprising in his love-play and feeling grateful he said:

"You can be sure that the promise I made to you will be kept. I have already forced Russia to give up the part she stole; time will do the rest. My first duty is to France then I shall restore Poland."

Marie was overjoyed and thought her sacrifice had not been in vain.

Unfortunately, a few hours later, Napoleon announced that he was leaving Warsaw. The young Pole burst into tears.

"Whatever will become of me?"

"You must come to Paris, sweet Marie, with the Grand Marshal as Guardian. He will look after you. You will only have to ask him and all your wishes will be met."

She repeated that her sole desire was that he should restore her country.

"All the treasures in the world could not satisfy me, nor restore my self-respect," she said. "Unless Poland is restored I shall go and live by myself in the country."

Napoleon became more affectionate.

"No Marie, I cannot have that. You are kind and gentle and your heart is pure. How can you think of depriving me of the few moments of happiness I have every day with you! You alone can give them to me."

Marie, in fond hopes of getting nearer to Napoleon, to whose charm she had begun to succumb, returned to Poland and stayed with her mother for three weeks.

After several nights, tossing in a cold bed and dreaming of passionate embraces, she threw on a bearskin cloak and a fur cap, jumped on a sleigh and sped away to the Castle of Finckenstein, where the Emperor had decided to spend the Winter.

There for three months they passed the sweetest and most exhausting of honeymoons.

Napoleon was seldom as happy as during this Finckenstein interlude.

For the first time in his life he was linked with a human being who was sweet, loving, docile, genuine, straightforward and entirely free from coquetry.

Marie died in December 1817, and according to her wishes her heart was placed in an urn and her body was eventually carried to her beloved Poland.

HENRY II OF FRANCE
AND DIANE DE POITIERS

François I of France was released from captivity in Spain, but he had to leave behind him his two sons, François and Henri, as hostages.

They were finally liberated after a diplomatic marriage was arranged between François I and Charles V's sister Eleanor.

She had fallen in love with the King during his imprisonment in Madrid.

The meeting of father, fiancée and sons at St. Jean de Luz was to have extraordinary consequences of a far-reaching nature.

When they had dutifully kissed their father, the little Princes were enveloped in the arms of the Court Ladies.

Henri was only eleven at the time, but he was particularly over-whelmed when a beautiful lady advanced to embrace him.

She was the wife of Louis de Brèze, *Comte* to Maulevrier, Grand Sénéchal of Normandy.

She was to be known to history by her maiden name, Diane de Poitiers.

Soon after the Coronation of Queen Eleanor, the young Princes took part in a tournament.

When they rode up to bow before the lady of their choice, Henri — to everybody's astonishment — lowered his standard before Diane who was seated with the other Court ladies, including Anne de Pisseleu, *Duchesse* d'Etampes, mistress of François I.

A competition was held at the end of the festivities to elect the loveliest woman of the day.

Half the votes went to Anne, and the other half to Diane who, at the age of thirty-two, should have been 'an old lady' according to the canons of the day.

Anne never forgave her.

Henri became more and more arduous.

His marriage to plain little Catherine de Medici did not alter his affection for Diane — perhaps it even increased it.

He continued to wear her colours (black and white) to call her his *dame* and to send her poems composed, not with the same delicate talent as his father, but with schoolboyish exaltation.

It was in his vivid imagination.

He was inclined to be dreamy and his early years spent in a dismal Spanish dungeon had accentuated this tendency.

He had read countless romances and was imbued with the ideals of medieval chivalry to a more chimerical extent than his father.

Diane was his 'far-away Princess' — the ideal *dame* for whom the romantic Prince secretly yearned.

She was the incarnation of a myth, a dream, and there could be no stronger tie.

It was not surprising that she reigned longer than any other Monarch's mistress.

Henri was the last Royal troubadour.

Diane soon knew that Catherine de Medici had no place in the affections of Henri.

He treated her with absolute indifference and lived elsewhere whenever it was possible to do so.

The real tragedy of Catherine's life which was not revealed until many years later, was that she had quickly fallen in love with her husband.

She would have done anything for him, just to have had a kindly gesture from him.

Diane was already thirty-one years old when she met the Prince and at that moment she changed the whole of his future life.

Home after so many years, and already speculation was beginning as to how the young Princes could be utilised in the future for the good of their country.

Diane heard an old man say that in his opinion a marriage would be useful and possibly essential.

Diane could hardly believe that she had heard yet another callous arrangement being made as regards the future life of the little boy of whom she had become very fond.

She however hid her affection from the King and her husband.

Only she knew how terribly the long years of imprisonment had affected Henri.

From his father he had inherited a powerful body, but from his mother, a fear of living.

He had no self-confidence, despite the fact that there was no horse he could not tame and no beast too dangerous for him to hunt.

He was afraid, however, of life as he found it at the French Court.

For four years he had awakened each day to the pattern of iron bars against the sky and had fallen asleep at night to the measured tread of brutal jailers.

Cruelties, jibes, hunger and fear had given him a strange melancholy.

"No one," the French Courtiers told each other, "could get at the heart of this timid youth."

King François had no patience with Henri.

He enjoyed the gaiety and charm of the Dauphin who was so like himself, but thought his younger son was sullen and morose.

The marriage negotiations were protracted and on one occasion virtually abandoned.

Diane could however give little attention between the slow hesitant haggling between France and the Papacy for it was obvious that her husband was dying.

Louis de Brèze was a man of quiet and unspectacular courage, as his military record had proved.

Now he accepted that death was approaching without fear or resistance against the inevitable.

Diane had never loved her husband more than when he was helpless and dependent upon her.

She not only cared for him, making herself nurse,

attendant and Valet, but also kept him alive with her optimism.

In July, 1531 Louis de Brèze died at the age of seventy-two.

The Funeral was carried out with great pomp and ceremony.

It was the convention at the time that the widow should be completely hidden from head to foot in layers of black garments which entirely disguised all shape and semblance of a human being.

Diane ordered a mourning costume of black and white which was every bit as becoming as any of her famous gowns of green.

It fitted closely to her body and had a bodice of exquisite white lace. Around each arm were bands in silver thread.

The black sleeves were slit to the elbow so that they fell away in folds and her forearms were covered in billowing white muslin.

Encircling Diane's waist was a silver chain and on her head she wore a black headdress.

She looked so lovely that she completely changed funereal fashions and a version of her dress became accepted for all high-born widows.

After the funeral ceremony, Diane had to remove her husband's entrails which were buried in the grounds of the Chapel at Anet.

She sent his heart to the Abbey where his murdered father and mother had been buried.

The body itself was interred in the Cathedral at Rouen.

Diane remained in virtual retirement at Anet for little more than a year.

It was at this time she became preoccupied with the fact that she was not only a widow, but at thirty-one years of age she was advancing quickly to what was in those days her declining years.

She was determined to sustain what had been such an asset to her − her beauty.

Summer and Winter alike during that year of mourning, she rose at three o'clock in the morning and bathed herself from head to foot in ice-cold well water, and also had something to drink.

There are many legends and stories about this draught. Some say it was a bouillon of liquid gold, others that it was a secret elixir which she had obtained from a wise woman.

In all probability it was soup or fruit juice.

Diane then went for a gallop on horseback which lasted, even if the weather was bad, for three hours.

By eight o'clock she was back in bed where she lay relaxing her body and reading, until midday.

Early in 1533, she let the King know that she was ready to accept his old invitation to join his band of twenty-seven honour-matrons at Court.

There was great excitement when it was known that the widowed Grand Sénéchale was coming, for the few who had visited her had brought back fantastic stories of her unbelievable beauty.

There was also much intriguing gossip that François had always seemed to be particularly attracted to Diane.

All that the Court had heard was more than borne out by the lovely young widow.

The brilliance of her conversation and her wit brought the Courtiers clustering round her, and her ability as a horsewoman delighted the King.

Diane was the King's close companion during many hours in which they would ride, however varied his companions at night might be.

She dared once to protest against the cold, calculating use of Henri as a piece on the Political chessboard, but the King did not listen.

He was too preoccupied with the sparring and arguing which would break out when he met the Pope.

Henri, obediently kept within earshot when the Pope arrived, but at no time were the boy's wishes brought into the conversation or discussion.

The best that he could do to acquaint himself with his future wife, Catherine de Medici, was to glance shyly towards the assembled Papal dignitaries and try to see the little girl who stood, diffident and frightened, somewhere at the rear amongst the female relatives.

If Henri and Catherine had not been so introspective, they would have found they had much in common.

Henri's childhood had, through force of war and Political negotiation, been unhappy. Catherine had suffered in much the same manner.

Her mother had died giving birth to her, and her father had died a week or two later.

The child became a puppet of warring Florentine factions.

An observant Ambassador said of Catherine:

"She is not pretty, for she has the big eyes and the thick lips of the Medicis, but she loves her husband as much as can be imagined."

Catherine's intelligent mind however served her well and the careful observations she made of how the ladies of the Court behaved enabled her to wriggle into the affections of her father-in-law.

She learnt how to dance gracefully, and dancing was something of which the King was very fond.

She also persisted with riding lessons so that she could emulate Diane, and although her ill-shaped little body looked very graceless and awkward she was woman enough to realise she had beautiful legs.

With a flash of inspiration, she had a special saddle made so that her skirts were caught up and her calves exposed.

Then suddenly, in 1536, the whole situation was changed.

The Dauphin, returning from military activities in Provence, stopped near Lyon to rest for a day or two before reporting to his father at Fontainbleau.

It was high Summer and after playing a violent game of tennis he asked for a glass of water.

It was brought to him full of ice conveyed from the Maritime Alps.

The Dauphin drank it down without stopping and died almost immediately afterwards.

Not unnaturally, the unfortunate Courier who had handed him the glass was accused of murder.

There seems however little doubt that the man was innocent of the charge brought against him and that the Dauphin died from an embolism caused by gulping lumps of ice into an overheated body.

The result of this tragedy was in one brief day to change the situation completely for Diane.

The boy she had loved as a child and who she was well aware still looked on her with adoration, was now heir to the throne of France.

The son of a King said to be dying from the excesses of his lifetime of debauchery.

It was inevitable that Diane's beauty should infuriate the women who were younger than her, but looked older.

François was in such a quandry that he appealed to Diane.

"The boy seems half dead!" he complained, "why should a son of mine find no savour in life?"

"Perhaps he needs to fall in love Sire," Diane answered.

The King gave a short laugh.

"That is another talent he has not inherited," he snorted. "He neither appeals to women, nor they to him. His manhood is as moribund as is his spirit."

"Not moribund, but asleep," Diane said quickly.

The King did not know, but Diane had for some time faced the most terrifying of human realities; the knowledge that she was necessary to no one.

Her husband was dead, her daughters were immersed in their education and she was clever enough to know how ephemeral was the favour of Kings and the adulation of Courtiers.

Her whole being craved love.

She knew it in the long dark nights when she could not sleep.

She knew it when the soft music of the Orchestra or the scent of flowers made her catch her breath.

She knew it when she . . .

Diane stopped suddenly.

The secret that had been hers for a long time made her afraid.

"I have never lived," she whispered to herself, remembering the eighteen years she had spent in Anet being dutiful to an old man who used her body when the urgency of desire was upon him, but left her unmoved and unawakened.

"Old, Old!"

She recalled the horror of the word when she had known she was to marry Louis de Brèze.

Now it was replaced by another word.

"Young, Young! too young!"

She had a sudden wild longing for her youth as she had never known it, for the strength and firmness of a young body.

For the lips that sought hers with the freshness of a man without great experience and for his hands which could be rough because youth was ardent and impatient.

"I love you! I worship you!"

She knew he would say just that — and mean it.

A boy who had never loved — a man as unawakened to passion as she herself!

Now because the King had spoken, Diane could face the sudden longing of her heart.

Dare she risk her security, her pride, her self-respect for love because that was what it amounted to.

Should she play safe, or should she give herself to the wild, heady ecstasy of living as she had never lived before?

Without saying good-bye to anyone Diane went to Chenonceau and while she walked by the river a Royal messenger came riding from Fontainbleau with a letter.

The dark red seal made her heart give a sudden leap.

She knew as she opened it that her fingers were trembling.

'I am like a girl with her first love letter,' she thought, but wonderingly and without scorn.

Slowly, savouring every word, she read:

"Madame I beg you to send me news of your health that I may act according to such news; for if you continue to be ill I should not wish to fail to come to you or to be of such service as I may.

In truth, I cannot live long without seeing you.

Because I am not afraid to risk the loss of my father's favour in order to be with you, honour me, I pray you, by granting my deep desire to serve you.

I assure you that I shall know little peace of mind until my Courier returns bringing me news of your health.

I beg you, therefore, to send me a true word as to how you do and when you will be able to depart.

I think you understand full well how little pleasure I have at Fontainbleau when I may not see you and that there is little happiness in life for me when I am absent from the one upon whom all my happiness depends.

Now I am not only unhappy but afraid that this letter be so long as to weary you in reading it, so that I commend to your indulgent care my humble homage which I beg you to cherish forever."

She raised her eyes.

The sun beyond the poplars was very bright and the glory of it filled her eyes.

She ran towards the house as if there were wings on her small feet.

She wrote only one line:

"I wait for you at Chenonceau."

Neither Diane nor the King gave a thought to Catherine.

Within days of Diane's returned from Chenonceau, it was noted by the Courtiers that Henri was staying at Court and for the first time, hunting and visits to Military establishments had been abandoned.

A new radiance about Diane and an understandable air of triumph exuding from Henri were clues enough for the busy-bodies whose main interest was to dig out scandal.

Diane one day moving through the Galerie des Cerfs at Fontainbleau heard the *Duchesse* d'Etampes say:

"It is witchcraft which explains *Madame* la Senechale's youth. She communicates with Satan, who keeps her young."

Diane knew she could not let this remark go unchallenged.

"This is ill done, *Madame* d'Etampes," she said angrily. "You do me foul wrong. Many have been your rudenesses. Now you are pleased to be malevolent. I beg you to believe that I do not commune with Satan. My youth is not a thing of witchcraft."

Unfortunately for Diane, the damage was done.

Her daily bathing in well water was well known and something she had never denied.

Some said the water must have some magical ingredient in it, while others said she preferred water drawn from the bowels of the earth from rain water or river water.

This could be a significant pointer to some alliance to the powers of the Underworld.

The *Duchesse's* personal theory was that Diane dissolved gold in the water she sponged on her face and body.

It was obvious to her that the elixir of life must have some connection with the untarnishable metal.

At the same time, no gold could be dissolved in water by human agency.

One afternoon at Fontainbleau the *Duchesse* was laughing in her hard, brittle tone as a Courtier recited the latest scurrilous lampoon that a Court hack had written about Diane.

Unnoticed Prince Henri walked into the room.

His pale face darkened as he listened.

He strode forward and as the women around the

Duchesse hurriedly stood up and curtsied to the Heir to the Throne, he said:

"The beauty of what you call 'Autumn' can eclipse the tawdry colours of Spring."

The *Duchesse* was nonplussed at being overheard.

She attempted to retrieve the situation by exclaiming:

"It is as I have said, the Dauphin is a victim of that woman's evil wiles. He is so bewitched that he cannot see the truth for himself, but pretends that age is more attractive than youth, Poor boy, I shudder for the fate of France. Fortunately, the King is aware of the position."

This was wishful thinking.

The King, if he were aware of the schisms which threatened his Kingdom, did not regard Diane as one of them.

Diane had never forgotten that the Kings of France must have an heir.

Diane set herself the unendurable task of helping Henri and Catherine to do their duty and produce an Heir to the Throne.

She loved Henri and she had not only awakened in him an emotion which consumed him like a burning flame, but had given him a confidence and a sense of responsibility which he had never had before.

But even as she answered his passion with passion and was thrilled and aroused by his youth and vigour as if they were the same age, she could never forget that Henri's first duty was to his country.

Henri had found in Diane those things that all men seek in the woman they love — mistress, mother, goddess.

Knowing this, she could never fail him — or allow him to fail himself.

Catherine had suffered much since her marriage.

She was humiliated by her husband's coldness and inattention.

She was insulted by the open acceptance of Diane's hold over him.

Yet, she did not, until much later in her life, show any hatred for her rival; nor did she ally herself on the side of the *Duchesse* d'Etampes.

Diane was well aware that Henri suffered from a physiological defect which made fruitful intercourse difficult, or even impossible.

That he could fertilize a woman had been supposedly proved in the past with a girl whom he was said to have given a baby.

This appeared to be a freakish exception.

Diane considered that not only would Henri continue to be frustrated if the minor surgery needed was not carried out, but she told Catherine that the absence of a legitimate child was his fault.

Her sense of justice as well as patriotism made her determined to put things right.

Few mistresses would have exercised their minds in order to make the sexual life of the lover's wife more satisfactory and fruitful.

Diane did this and much more.

Her purpose was not wholly disinterested, for she badly wanted the line of the throne to be safely secured through Henri's son.

She persuaded Henri to have the operation.

At the same time, she had a woman-to-woman talk with Catherine.

The 'poor little Italian', as the Court called her disparagingly, was so desolated at her failure to conceive after four years of marriage that she was ready to accept advice from anyone.

Diane then learnt with horror of the bizarre and nauseating potions the quacks Catherine employed had suggested to her.

The unfortunate young woman was managing to drink the urine of pregnant animals.

She was swallowing potions composed of the dried and powdered sexual organs of the wild boar, stag and domestic cat.

Herbs crushed on her food and dissolved in wine were drank in great quantities.

Having confessed all this the tearful girl then undressed to show Diane the religious emblems suggested by her priests, with the middle finger and the anus of a foetus born two months before its time, hanging incongruously from a girdle of goat's hair made by a witch.

Diane, a deeply religious woman, told the Queen to remove the religious and magical symbols from her body and to pray ceaselessly.

She then gave her some practical advice on love-making which was new to Catherine.

By discreet questioning, she discovered, as she expected, that in her conjugal relationship with her husband Catherine had never experienced proper intercourse.

She heartened the girl by telling her – and by this time hypocrisy about the relationship between Henri and Diane was pointless – that she had persuaded Henri to have an operation.

She said she firmly believed that this would eradicate the chief defect and it would be up to Catherine to deal with any others.

The room where Diane slept was immediately below the Queen's bedchamber.

On many nights when Henri came to Diane's arms she would allow him to make love to her and return his passionate advances.

Then quite suddenly and with an abruptness which hid her own yearnings and desire for him, she would say:

"Now go to your Consort and lie with her."

Time after time she made this sacrifice.

The little-boy and older-woman relationship which there had been from the beginning of their acquaintance with one another had never entirely left Henri.

His instinct to obey her was more powerful than his manly desire.

Very rarely did he ignore the command and with hungry

lips stifle the words as Diane endeavoured to repeat them.

From the Royal purse there came later a gift to Diane of a five-thousand, five-hundred *livres* an official present registered in the records of the Royal Exchequer.

The reason for it was set down:

"For the good and commendable services the Comtesse de Daint-Vallier hath before this done for the welfare of the Queen."

The reward was justified.

In the Summer of 1541 Catherine could tell her husband that she was pregnant. Her son, the new Dauphin, François, was born on February 10th, 1542.

For ten years afterwards twelve months never passed without a further birth.

Catherine's fecundity made little difference to his feelings for her.

His indifference and disregard even of the privilges she deserved as his Consort and the mother of his children could be excused to some extent.

For hardly had she recovered from the birth of one child and been churched to permit her return to Court society than she had to retire once more as an expectant mother.

Catherine however privately found her new situation as galling as when she had felt she was a failure.

Diane had finally become his mistress, after thirty-nine years of an irreproachably virtuous life, in the Château d'Ecouen, to which both she and Henri had been invited by the Grand Maitre Anne de Montmorency.

This was a well-known 'obscene' Château whose coloured glass windows portrayed such daring erotic scenes that the 'light blushed to have to reveal them'.

Catherine de Medici was determined to discover the bewitching 'love technique' used by her rival.

She had the ceiling above Diane's room at the Palace pierced by several holes.

She saw a very beautiful, white, delicate and fresh woman, half-naked, clad in a chemise, caressing her lover with a wealth of charm and delicious folly, which her lover returned, until they slid from the bed on to the floor and, still in their chemises, pursued their gymnastics on the carpet, so avoiding the heat of the bed, for it was in the middle of a very warm Summer.

Sexual technique however was not the hold Diane had over Henri.

Henri regarded Catherine as a breeding machine and little more.

Henri never had any children by Diane.

She must have been cautious and well-informed for her time because we find a renowned Doctor dedicated his book on women's ailments to her.

François I died in 1547.

For his Coronation Henri called for the priests to display before him the robes and regalia which he saw were worn and shabby.

He ordered new ones to be made.

For the doublet he ordered an emblem of three crescents intertwined and carrying a cipher consisting of a double D linked and joined by an H.

This is probably the first occasion when the notorious, and later glorious, cipher was used.

It was a boyish, perhaps even pathetic display of adoration — a Royal and splendid version of the same impulse which makes other callow youths scribble their feelings on walls or on the trunks of trees.

Henri went further in the early weeks of his Kingship.

He called Architects to instruct them to prepare plans for rebuilding and extending the Palace of Saint Germain-en-Laye.

He made only one stipulation: the completed building should include the long, narrow Palace already existing, connected at both ends by a semi-circle.

The first new Palace of his reign must be in the shape of a letter D.

Only one more symbol of loyal favour and of passionate

love Henri had placed upon Diane's Coat-of-Arms his own heraldic device:

"DONC TOTUM IMPLEAT ORBUM' interpreting the phrase as 'My devotion shall be known throughout the world."

Henri was crowned King in Rheims on June 20th, 1547.

Diane had no official position at the outset but was an important member of the King's Privy Council, and its members, as well as its master, were largely controlled by her.

Many Kings' mistresses corrupted their lovers missions and brought ruin to the people they governed.

Historians have described the reign of Henri II of France as one of the most remarkable in French history, typified by national and international policy that was wise, just and far-seeing.

In a brilliant pen portrait of the French King Matteo Dandolo the Venetian Ambassador writes:

"His Majesty is in his twenty-ninth year and to-day I must assure you that he has become less melancholy, has a ruddy complexion and is in excellent health . . . His body is well-proportioned, tall rather than short. In his person he is full of courage, daring and is very enterprising . . . He is one of the most famous of swordsmen and in jousting, always accompanied by danger, he carries himself most valorously . . .

One can see Diane de Poitier's influence in this transformation.

One can also see how Henri longed to assert himself and be a conqueror if only in games and sport.

There was also another reason for such physical energy — Henri was very much in advance of his century in that he was afraid of getting fat.

He ate frugally and watched his figure anxiously.

Before him he had always the slim, exquisitely graceful Diane, not only in person, but in the portraits, bronzes, statues, enamels which were beginning to decorate the

Palace everywhere he looked.

So grateful was Henri for the able manner in which Diane piloted him in the first difficult months of his reign that he sought avidly for a way to show publicly his regard for her.

An easily arranged gesture was to restore the titles, taxes and duties of the Duchy of Valentinois which for three centuries had been forfeit by her family through unpaid debts.

Next, both his Ministers and his mistress were staggered by the token of esteem which he smilingly described as a 'nosegay which I want to lay at your feet'.

It consisted of a special levy called *'La Paulette*. This was by tradition a Royal prerogative, never hitherto bestowed on anyone not a member of the reigning House.

It permitted the person holding it to have the right to confirm all offices of the realm at the beginning of a new reign and receive payment in varying degrees for each position.

The value of this privilege was, of course, fantastic.

Everyone paid, from those of high rank in the State, officers gazetted into the Army, livings in the Church, down to minor officials in provinces, towns and on Royal estates.

The monies received from *La Paulette* had always been a lucrative source of revenue to the Royal families without, of course, involving unpopular matters of taxation.

Henri knew that Diane would not abuse the gift in any manner.

She was perfectly aware of the amount of money that was involved even in organizing it fairly and honestly, for she must have known what her father and husband had paid at the beginning of a new reign in connection with their own State offices.

Henri's generosity in simply handing over this right to her and calling it a little bunch of flowers staggered her.

"You are all goodness to me, Sire," she said, "but this

seems to me to be all too great a gift."

Henri, embarrassed by her gratitude said:

"My father was generous to many, I shall reward but a few."

Together Henri and Diane had much more than sex to bind them closer and still closer.

They studied, taking it in turns to read aloud to each other. They learned foreign languages, patronised artists, sculptors and culture which had been started by King François.

In fact they surrounded themselves with such beauty that visitors from other lands gasped in amazement at the treasures of the French Court.

Then suddenly it seemed as if Diane was a woman with the usual feminine emotions of jealousy and revenge.

The *Duchesse* d'Etampes was ordered to return the jewels she had received from François.

She was then banished from Court and stripped of all her titles.

She was told that, provided she remained on her estates she would not be molested.

The *Duchesse* was then forty years of age and growing fat, but still highly attractive, with her blonde hair and rosy-tinted skin.

Now at last she was powerless.

. . . . . .

Once again, the bugles were sounding in France to call men to arms.

Henri put on his armour to go at the head of the forces.

For Diane this was a time for sorrow rather than excitement.

She resorted to prayers as a means of protecting her beloved Henri.

She made pilgrimages to Holy places in North-West France and did constant penance by following a simple diet, cutting down her hours of rest and abstaining from luxurious clothing.

After a visit to Chartres Cathedral she sent Henri a replica of the chemise which was kept there and which was said to have been worn by the Madonna.

This was regarded as the reason why Chartres had many times withstood sieges and escaped destruction by fire.

When Henri wrote to thank her he signed the letter with a 'double D' signature and added:

"I beg you, M'ayme, to be willing to wear the enclosed ring for the love you bear me."

A tournament had been arranged to take place and Catherine sought an audience with Henri.

At dawn she was admitted to his bedchamber and was astonished when she burst into tears and begged him not to take part in the jousting.

At first he could not understand her reasoning and then, when he realised that she thought he would risk his life, he exclaimed:

"By the heavens! You have been listening to that lily-livered fellow Gausico, the Astrologer, who accosted me some weeks ago with a dismal tale."

"No only Luigi Gausico has warned me," the Queen replied, "I sent also for Nostradamus and he foretells 'death from a wound inflicted by cold steel during a duel.'"

"A duel, says he?" the King laughed. "Then I must take heart for a tourney is no duel."

He was right in this for the object of a tourney was to unhorse one's opponent, not to kill or disable him.

On each day of the tournament Catherine pleaded with him not to fight, but Henri was delighted with his success not least because many of those with whom he jousted were much younger than him.

The lists had been constructed in exactly the same place as those which had been used to celebrate the marriage of François I, when the young Prince Henri had first asked for and worn the green-and-white favours of Diane.

He was still wearing his mistress's emblem on this occasion although now the colours were white and black.

Diane sat in a more important position on the stand than she had twenty-four years ago, but a few who had attended both events told the younger neighbours who crowded around them that the *Duchesse* d'Valentinois, now close on sixty, looked very little different from when she was thirty-five.

Henri indulged in the jousting with consummate skill and ability and proved to an excited, cheering audience that he had, indeed, developed into a warrior King.

On the third day of the tournament, June 30th, 1559, he offered combat to his new brother-in-law, the *Duc* de Savoie.

This was to be the greatest event in the whole tournament.

Enormous crowds watched their King ride out from his pavilion on his favourite horse − *Compère*.

Twice he jousted and twice he was victorious.

He was waiting to enter the lists for the third time when the aged Marshal de Vieilleville begged an audience.

"I swear to God, Sire," he said, "that on three successive nights I have dreamed the same woeful dream. It has held the vision of a youth carrying a broken, bloody sword and crying out − 'The King is dead!'. By the Mass, I beg you not to ride again to-day."

"But on the faith of a true Knight," the King replied, "I have scarcely loosened my limbs. Bring me another lance for I will break one more before we depart."

Closing his vizor, Henri turned his horse and took the field.

His opponent was the Captain of the Scottish Palace guard, a young man named Gabriel Montgomery.

As the King charged his adversary so a strange preminition passed through the crowd.

Up till then there had been a bedlam of noise from trumpets and drums and the mob of Paris shouting encouragement.

Now everyone was silent.

Henri was getting tired and though each broke his lance, Montgomery unseated the King. He reeled in the saddle, but so cleverly did he manage his horse that he recovered from the blow and the crowd roared their delight.

It was the normal custom for a broken lance to be immediately thrown to the ground, but Montgomery was slow in doing this.

His horse carried him forward with the jagged stump of the broken shaft held a little above the horizontal.

The two horses passed each other and the end of the lance struck the King's head.

Apparently Henri's helmet had been slightly damaged in a previous combat and the vizor did not shut properly.

The broken end of the lance went through the gap and penetrated the King's skull just at the corner of the right eye, splintering the bone.

Compère, accustomed to the routine of jousting, continued on his way to the end of the list, while Henri, the sight of his right eye gone and the other blinded by blood, fell forward clasping his horse's neck.

At the exit the grooms rushed forward, lifted the King from the saddle and removed his helmet.

It was seen that Henri was seriously injured and had fainted.

In the Royal tribune, the Queen called out hysterically, the honour-maids screamed with fear and the Dauphin lost consciousness.

Diane, deathly pale, but outwardly calm, tried to climb over the railings to get to the King.

Her foot caught in the silver fringe of the cipher-woven hangings and she would have fallen if the Cardinal de Guise had not helped her to the ground.

By now the crowds had swarmed on to the ground and it was impossible for her to force her way through them.

Finally, she was taken home where she vainly tried to obtain information about the King.

Henri was taken to the Palace on a litter and carried to

his bedroom.

In spite of an agony of pain he sent for Montgomery and assured him the injury was an accident and he would suffer no harm because of it.

A surgeon probed in the wound and managed to remove several pieces of splintered bone but, because of the thinness of the bone at this point where the lance had entered, the blow had driven several tiny fragments into the brain.

Within twenty-four hours the distortion to the King's face indicated that an interior abcess had formed. Any efficacious method of treating this was quite unknown to the surgeons handling the case.

In an endeavour to ascertain where the offending pieces of bone might be and how close they were to the brain and vital nerves they had four criminals awaiting execution beheaded so that they could experiment on their skulls.

The jagged lance of Montgomery which had caused the injury was driven into each of the skulls and these were then opened and the position of the splinters studied.

All this was useful in theory, but valueless in practice. The pain which Henri suffered was almost unbearable.

The abcess grew larger and poisoned the blood system causing delirium and fever.

After four days the abcess burst and this gave the dying man some relief. It also caused his delirium to abate.

In the hour of coherent consciousness which was given to him he called for the Queen and made her swear she would see that his will and testament was carried out and that the loyal oath would be sworn by his heir upon his succession.

He ordered her to assist in every way she could their eldest son in the administration of his Kingdom and added that he knew that his own life was nearly over.

Diane suffered a mental torture which was insupportable in the thought that Henri not only needed her, but was being wrongly treated.

The idea of him in pain was bad enough, but to learn from her maids at Court that the doctors were ineffectual and unable to cure him, made her walk her bedchamber with tears streaming down her cheeks and her hands raised in supplication to Heaven.

At the end of two days of fruitless waiting she went to the Palace and begged admission to the King.

Defiantly the Queen refused her requests and Diane did not learn until much later that Henri had held on to consciousness in a desperate effort to see her before his confession was heard.

But he was too ill to insist that she be brought to him and he received the last Rites of the Catholic Church after which there was no question of him seeing the woman with whom he had committed 'mortal sin' for nearly a quarter of a century.

At long last Catherine had her husband — the King of France — to herself.

Diane returned to her house which was only a few yards away and spent the hours both day and night either praying or sitting at the window where she could watch what was happening at the doorway of the Palace on the other side of the road.

She could hardly believe this was not a dream.

It seemed to her now that nothing could hurt more than that Henri should be stricken and helpless and that she could not be there to comfort and sustain him as she had done all through the years they had been together.

After a week a messenger came from Catherine bearing an order to Diane to return the Crown Jewels.

She felt a clammy fear clutching at her heart and her hands went cold.

"Is the King dead?" she enquired.

"No, *Madame,*" he replied, "but it is believed he will not live the day."

Diane felt a surge of relief and with it her pride and courage returned.

"So long as there remains in His Majesty an atom of life," she said, "I would wish that my enemies know that I have no fear of them. As yet I have no master. I am still of good courage, When the King is dead I do not wish to live after him, and all the bitterness that my enemies would wish me will be but sweetness beside my grief."

The atom of life remained in the King's valiant body, but so tiny that it was hardly identifiable.

The abcess had renewed itself and grew larger.

Henri lost the power of speech and paralysis was creeping over his body.

The last few days he was in a deep coma until at noon, twelve days after he had been wounded, one of his doctors held a silver mirror above his mouth.

There was no misting.

On July 12th, 1559, wrote Vieilleville, *"God's will was done. At one hour after noon the King lay dead."*

Hardly had the sun risen over the roofs of Paris before Catherine's messenger was hammering on the door of Diane's house, repeating the demand of the return of the jewels.

Diane was also ordered to hand over the duplicate keys of the King's cabinets and desk which contained State papers, and to display all her jewels so that those which were Crown property could be taken should she have omitted to include them in the casket which she had already prepared against the expected demand.

With great dignity, her face like a mask and her eyes dark with suffering, she did as she was ordered.

In her heart she understood the Queen's rage for, as someone wrote:

"Diane had robbed her of her husband for the whole of her reign in the sight and knowledge of everyone."

Quietly Diane packed and left with dignity and without haste, as befitted her rank.

The only thing she carried personally was a box containing Henri's letters and the poems he wrote to her.

She had read and re-read them these past days until, because of her tears, she could no longer see the words.

At Anet, where she and Henri had known more happiness than is ever given to human beings Diane felt a sudden indescribable peace.

Diane died after a short illness and without pain on a day when spring covered her beautiful garden with blossom.

It was April 25th, 1566 and she was sixty-six years of age. Six months before her death Brantôme wrote:

". . . she is still so beautiful that there is no heart of stone that would not be moved. She is of the most perfect whiteness without using any cosmetic . . ."

The funeral was expected to be quiet, but when her death became known, nobles, officials and former friends came flocking to Anet from all over France.

The garden was a miracle of colour and blossom. It seemed incredible that they would not see Diane moving across the velvet green lawns to greet them − her face as young, lovely and expectant as the spring itself.

The mourning pall marked with the Royal cipher moved slowly past Jean Goujon's glorious statue of Diane as the Huntress, past Jean Nicole's exquisite fountain where she stood beneath the iridescent water and into the Chapel carved everywhere with Ds and Hs indivisibly intertwined.

The murmur of the mourners filled the building and echoed across the sun-filled garden.

It percolated the whole wonder and beauty of the Château d'Anet.

'Priez Dieu pour Diane de Poitiers.'

KING HENRY II AND DIANE DE POITIERS

PRINCE SI AHMED AND AURÉLIE PICCARD
1849-1929

Aurélie Piccard, a little provincial French girl was born in 1849 in Montigny-le-Roi in Northern France.

Her father had served in the Army during the French conquest of Algeria.

The family then moved to another little town, Arc-en-Barrois, where, with many younger brothers and sisters to be fed, Aurélie went out to work at fifteen.

She was neat-fingered and quick, and soon made herself indispensable to the Milliner to whom she was apprenticed.

It was a hard existence and Aurélie dreamed of escape to glowing horizons.

The only colour in her life was when her father recounted his adventures in North Africa.

She listened rapturously to stories of the desert of Moorish Palaces, charging Arab warriors, and blazing stars.

It all became part of her dreams.

She left the Milliner's establishment to better herself as a Housekeeper in the Château of Arc-en-Barrois, property of the Prince de Joinville, but leased to a député of the Haute Marne, a *Monsieur* Steenackers.

His wife took a fancy to the girl, and soon Aurélie found herself installed as *dame de compagnie*.

It was certainly a change because she was allowed to ride the fine horses in the stables and became an excellent horsewoman.

In 1871, came the Franco-Prussian war and almost the only means of communication with Paris was by carrier-pigeon, messages being sent regularly to and from the besieged Capital by this means.

In his official capacity as *Directeur Général des Postes, Monsieur* Steenackers received all such messages.

The pigeons were first brought to Aurélie who detached

the tiny cylinders and took them to her master.

She also looked after the birds and one day, as she stood among the swooping multitude, an impressive figure in Arab dress approached.

His costume was magnificent.

A dark *burnouse* was flung over another white one, and that over a white robe belted with a silk scarf, through which was thrust a jewel-handled dagger.

His boots were of soft crimson leather spurred with gold, and pinned to his robe were a number of orders and decorations, some of which Aurélie recognised as French.

As he approached her she was aware of a heady perfume coming from him so that he seemed to move in an exotic aura.

This remarkable personage was surrounded by an entourage of guards, black slaves, Courtiers, and interpreters.

The next day, and for several days following he reappeared, silent, but fixing Aurélie with a gaze that was romantic and admiring.

It seemed to her as if he thought she was some celestial vision.

She was unaware that because she was so fair-skinned and surrounded by the pigeons which were venerated by the Moslems as sacred, she did actually seem that to him.

Curious, Aurélie learned that her admirer was Prince Si Ahmed Tedjani, a young Arab Ruler from Southern Algeria who, with his half-brother Si Bachir had for some time been an object of attention in Governmental circles.

He had been given a standing ovation when attending the Opera from the Préfet's box.

Public enthusiasm was great, for the feudal Arab chiefs had offered their allegiance and support to the hard-pressed French.

The Algerians found French domination infinitely preferable to the Turkish yoke, even though the Turks were of the same religion as themselves.

Prince Si Ahmed was as excitable as his appearance.

He was the child of Sudanese slave-girl and the Shareef of the Tedjanis, the mightly Prince Si Mohammed-Seghir, the *Marabout* and absolute Ruler of the Tedjanis.

These were a religious sect, one of many throughout Northern Africa.

The slave-girl, though pregnant by the Prince, had left his Harem to follow another master, which was not unusual.

She vanished and nothing more would ever have been heard of her or her child had not Si Mohammed-Seghir died suddenly, leaving among all his wives and concubines only one sickly baby son.

The Tedjani nobles were worried that their dynasty rested with one frail boy, and when it was remembered the slave-girl had borne a son, they dispatched messengers in search of her.

When at last she and her child were found, it was a robust little boy of seven who was brought back in triumph to the *Xaouia,* to be installed in state beside his half-brother, the weakling si Bachir.

Between them the two Princes were co-heirs to the absolute power and glory accorded to Shareefs.

This, then, was the over-whelming person whom Aurélie Piccard had captivated.

First by her blonde charms and later by her force of character.

To begin with the courtship was very difficult as they had no common language.

The presence of an interpreter did not make things easy for one so passionately enamoured as the Prince.

Aurélie met his advances with down-cast eyes, but her modest calm concealed a turmoil of fears and hopes.

Here was the means of realising her wildest dreams.

Aurélie glanced occasionally at him from beneath her long lashes and the Prince could think of nothing else.

Accompanied by his Suite, the Prince made a formal

call on *Madame* Steenackers to ask Aurélie's price.

He was prepared to pay anything for such a treasure — absolutely anything!

"But Aurélie is not for sale!" replied the astonished *Madame* Steenackers. "She is not for sale."

The Prince paled until the Depute's wife explained that Aurélie could be married, but nothing else.

"So be it!" replied the Prince.

If that was the custom, he would marry *Mademoiselle* Piccard, now at once. Tonight.

It was with reluctance that the Prince left for his own apartments and in agitation, the Steenackers sent for Aurélie's father.

By now the whole place was in a ferment, for Aurélie announced that she would accept the Prince's proposal.

Spurred on by love, the Prince was making rapid progress with his French, although his exotic reputation and the splendid jewels he wore and lavished on Aurélie must have been a more powerful argument than any words for the girl from Arc-en-Barrois.

It was quite useless for anyone to advise her to be prudent. She already recognised the depths of the Prince's protestations of devotion.

Her own feelings for him were growing.

Above all, through him, she would be able to reach Africa, and the world that her father's stories had made it seem to her like Fairyland.

It was finally decided that the marriage should take place in Algiers, under French Law and when the Prince and his Suite sailed for Marseilles Aurélie and *Monsieur* Piccard went with them.

At that time, Algeria consisted only a French Barracks and Military Headquarters grouped round the harbour, although a new European town was planned beside the Cathedral.

The entire Piccard family, as well as Aurélie and her father, were treated by Si Ahmed as his own people and installed in a splendid Arab house he had acquired for them.

Here Aurélie began to learn some Arabic.

Already she loved the graceful, unhurried life in the beautiful old house with its patios and fountains, its shimmering blue and green tile work and the dim rooms shaded from the glare by fretted *mouchrabiyehs*.

The few, but rich pieces of furniture, low tables and coffers, were of cedarwood inlaid with mother-of-pearl.

The hanging lamps were of chased silver, and the divans were deep in cushions.

Musk and sandalwood perfumed the rooms and countless slaves were always at hand, bringing trays of strangely spiced foods, or filling the coffers with more and more of the sumptuous trappings which were to adorn Aurélie as the Prince's bride.

Suddenly Aurélie's happiness was shattered.

The French Governor-General refused to sanction a Franco-Arab union.

There was no provision for it in French Law.

He was unsympathetic and obdurate and all the Piccards' pleadings fell on deaf ears.

Aurélie wept and the Prince raged, threatening to raise a Tedjani insurrection.

The Officials remained adamant. Aurélie remained firm — marriage, or nothing.

The deadlock dragged on miserably until at last she faced an humiliating return to Arc-en-Barrois, where the pitying or spiteful looks of the neighbours were inevitable.

She pleaded with her father for more time, but the Piccards were proud.

Their daughter could not go round begging for some native's favours.

They would sail on the next ship and all the jewels would be given back.

Aurélie wept and the Prince pleaded.

Then fate stepped in, this time as Cardinal Lavigerie,

the Archbishop of Algiers.

He was just beginning his great missionary work in North Africa.

He was both visionary and practical.

The plight of the thwarted lovers interested him. He had noticed the unhappy girl who came to pray in his Church.

In these two people he saw the embodiment of his ideal for a Franco-Arab unity.

The Cardinal sent for Si Ahmed and realising the young Prince could be transformed into a powerful ally or an implacable enemy, he promised on certain conditions to perform the marriage himself.

French officials warned Aurélie she would forfeit her birthright. She could no longer look to them if things went wrong.

The Prince was overcome with gratitude and gave his word to the Archbishop.

He would marry Aurélie as his only wife.

From that moment, he was always to prove himself loyal to France, always to aid Aurélie in her efforts to further French influences, and to promote peaceful relations.

The simple marriage ceremony was performed by the Cardinal in his Chapel of Saint Eugene.

Then a great cortege formed outside Si Ahmed's house.

The Tedjanis were escorting their Shareef and his bride back to Aim Mahdi.

The camels were loaded up with all the baggage of tents and rugs, provisions and cooking utensils and painted coffers topped by Aurélie's European trunks and hat boxes.

As an Arab woman she should have followed her lord and master in a close-curtained litter slung across a camel which is the traditional mode of travel for Arab women.

But with the brilliant instinct which had always guided her, Aurélie now made a tremendous decision.

No veils, no traditions for her. She would begin as she meant to go on.

It was a clever move for it proved how original she was.

The enraptured Prince could refuse her nothing.

Mounted on a white Arab mare saddled in velvet with coral and silver trappings, Aurélie rode out to meet her future, unveiled, beside, not following her husband.

It took nearly a month to reach their destination because at that time there were no roads, and the caravan moved slowly in the blazing sun.

They went towards glittering mirages and through blinding storms, accompanied by a fierce, suffocating wind until suddenly a stillness falls and there is peace.

Then a sunrise or sunset of ineffable beauty suffuces everything and the desert seems reborn.

Aurélie fell deeply under the spell of the land with every mile she rode, and loved it all.

In the evening, when the tents were pitched and the camels, snarling and growling lay down, she knew how rapturously happy she was in this new life with her adoring husband.

This was her honeymoon, and her love for him joined her love for the desert.

When the huge stars glittered above them and the Prince lay beside her, passionate and loving, he had a rival.

It was the desert.

The desert possessed Aurélie, bringing her closer and closer to the fate she had been aware of so many years earlier.

She began to understand the full, mystical significance of her husband's Shareefan title and the degree of respect and veneration in which he was held.

In France he had appeared a Princely figure – in Algeria he was a grand Seigneur, accorded special prestige among so many other Arab nobles.

All along the way to the wells, nomads swarmed around them to kiss the hem of his robes and to prostrate themselves, or clutch at his stirrup, imploring the maraboutic blessing which he was divinely endowed to bestow.

Si Ahmed was of the noblest Shareegan blood which, in Islam, ranks higher than any other, for he traced his ancestry back to Idriss, son of Fatma Zorah, the Prophet's daughter.

He had an unassailable position, and Aurélie knew she must maintain not only her hold on him, but also the loyalty of his followers.

However sumptuous Si Ahmed's possessions had seemed, his costumes and jewels, his weapons, horses such as Aurélie had known in Algiers, Ain Mahdi came as a rude awakening.

Besides the grim appearance of the fortress there was a mixture of opulence and decay that was typically Arab.

Bats had taken over the falling rafters where the lovely painted ceilings had crumbled, doors hung on rusted chimneys and rats had chewed the magnificent rugs.

In the court-yard enormous cauldrons used to feed the household, the slaves and the ceaseless flow of pilgrims who passed through the *Zaouia* were blackened with rancid grease.

Even the Mausoleum of Si Ahmed's father was musty and neglected and the green standards of the Prophet hung in tatters over his Tomb.

Only the foundations lisped softly in the arcaded inner courts of the Harem to where Aurélie was conducted in state, and waited, behind its heavily barred doors and windows, to be greeted by her new family — her mother-in-law, the former Sudanese slave-girl, and her fourteen sisters-in-law, daughters of Si Ahmed's father by another wife.

At once, as if invested with some spiritual faculties, or guided by a strange prescience, this inexperienced girl took control.

She started to set both the Harem and the *Zaouia* to rights.

The Prince's wives and concubines were banished, pensioned off and honourably discharged.

At once her new family doted on her.

The Sudanese mother-in-law and the fourteen sisters-in-law, like the slaves, marvelled as she opened the barred doors of the Harem, coming and going as she pleased — and unveiled.

The slaves, Dongolo negresses, scattered to do her bidding and the dignitaries of the *Zaouia* respected her on sight.

Only her brother-in-law, Si Bachir remained hostile, jealously observing her hold, not only over Si Ahmed, but the entire complex of Ain Mahdi.

Aurélie once again showed that intuition or perception which had guided her in her new life.

She could not know at that moment that she would remain childless, that again her hopes for an heir would be dashed.

Yet on her wish, a little boy, Si Ali, the Prince's child by one of the concubines, remained at Ain Mahdi, to be loved and brought up as her own.

Barren women are soon repudiated by Arab custom, but Aurélie's supremacy was never to be challenged by her Tedjanis.

It was Allah's will that *Lallah Yamina,* as they called her, should come to direct their lives, and it was Allah's will, too, that she was childless.

She was a being apart, celestial, both for her adoring husband and his people.

At Ain Mahdi, all Aurélie's French sense of thrift and good management was displayed.

Soon, the withered gardens bloomed and the household accounts tallied.

The slaves were initiated in how to use a flat-iron and were soon laundering Aurélie's complicated underwear.

She continued to wear European clothes with buttons, basques and whalebones, for Si Ahmed now showed a marked preference for every manifestation of European living — including champagne.

This was in defiance of the Koranic vetoes.

Since he was so venerated, however, the Faithful held that on his lips alcohol became milk, and any signs of excess were attributed to mystic exaltation.

Aurélie turned one of the tile-dadoed rooms into her bedroom and installed a double bed of European design.

There, once buttoned into her long-sleeved nightgown, lying between smooth linen sheets, she was joined by Si Ahmed.

She soon realised how much prestige these foreign habits gave her and continued them long after she would have preferred to adopt local traditions.

In the years ahead, she made a number of journeys to Algiers to load up trains of camels with grand pianos, crystal chandeliers, billiard tables and whole satin-covered suites of gilt furniture.

To Arab eyes they breathed splendour and strangeness.

She never stayed away long, hurrying back to the desert as to a lovers rendezvous.

She adored the spreading Tedjani lands.

All, all must come under her hand.

Backed by bemused Si Ahmed she summoned French engineers and agricultural experts.

Tracts of waste land were irrigated, wells were sunk, new crops sewn. Hygiene and medicine saved many lives.

Everything she did for the benefit of Tedjani territories, *her* lands, *her* people.

She was the *Princesse des Sables,* her powers extending into the lunar landscape of the Hoggar.

In everything her husband stood beside her, the mighty Shareef, guiding, controlling, possessing, living an inner life of love where no one else could follow.

Si Ahmed kept the promises he had made to the Cardinal. There was never any question of him taking another wife, or of Aurélie's supremacy being challenged.

Thus the years of love, power and achievement passed for Aurélie, living her Saharan idyll.

In 1883 she set about building sumptuous new domain seven miles distant at Kourdane where a great pistachio tree grew beside a little spring.

Kourdane was once a Prince's Palace, a rural retreat and an agricultural experiment.

All the Saharan chiefs came there on visits of ceremony and curiosity, so did the French-Generals, Governor-Generals, deputes, explorers, all found their way to Kourdane, to be received with princely hospitality.

There was only one shadow over this golden scene.

Si Ali, the Shareef's heir, had turned out badly. He was lazy and he drank.

In 1887 the Tree of Paradise shivered and Si Ahmed's leaf fell when on a visit to the Tedjani *Zaouiias* of Tunis, he died unexpectedly of blood poisoning.

It was a profound shock for Aurélie. They had been together for so many marvellous years, and he was not yet fifty.

Moreover, since he had died away from Ain Mahdi, his body, by custom, must remain where he died, thus transferring all the Shareefan glory and substance of Ain Mahdi to follow his body.

Aurélie battled with the authorities to have this changed and because she was European her efforts at last prevailed.

Si Ahmed's body was brought back to the Kourdane where, in the gardens he had loved, she built a simple and beautiful red marble *Koubbah* as his monument.

Now Aurélie had no more part to play in Tedjani affairs and found that her days at Kourdane were numbered, since Si Bachir was determined on her departure.

She had imagined that Kourdane, her own creation would remain hers. Not so, and Si Bachir determined on her banishment, not only from Ain Mahdi but from Kourdane too.

Aurélie faced parting both from her life's work and the Pavilion of her heart. As withdrawn in grief as in joy, she retreated to Algiers.

Yet again, for the third time, Fate stepped in to change her fortune.

For some time she had been tormented by hearing from passing Tedjanis of the disorder and decay to which Si Bachir's indifference and ineffectual rule had reduced both Ain Mahdi and Kourdane.

Gradually the Tedjanis began to realise that Aurélie's presence was vital to their prosperity.

At the same moment the French administration was becoming uneasy at a growing turbulence and lack of co-operation among the tribes.

They hit on a most ingenious plan, and proposed that Aurélie should contract a marriage with Si Bachir, thus returning Ain Mahdi to be once more officially associated with the *Zaouia* and all its politics.

In spite of their dislike of each other both Aurélie and Si Bachir consented to this arrangement, for it was to their mutual benefit.

The marriage took place before the Caid of El Aghouat, Aurélie now taking a particular pleasure in declining the civil marriage which, at last, after many years, the French authorities pressed on her.

Her return to Ain Mahdi was triumphant, amid scenes of touching devotion from the Tedjanis.

Having become once more the wife of a Shareef, she could resume her life's work.

She and Si Bachir had agreed to go their separate ways, he to follow the old idling pattern, she to order and restore the Tedjani affairs.

Kourdane, she decided should be her headquarters, and with a lover's impatience, she set out once more to cross the arid track that lay between her and her adored.

Even in the short time she had been away the beautiful gardens had been destroyed and the house had become a tarnished mockery of its former glory.

Aurélie, however, was an undaunted and energetic fifty years of age.

With a lover's devotion she set about restoring it, and soon it was as before; but now, all hers, doubly precious for the time of separation she had suffered.

For twelve years more Aurélie lived her Saharan love affair with Kourdane, and the marvellous desert from which it had grown. She sought no other company, although she was still received in style.

She no longer ate with her guests, joining them for coffee, but taking her meals in her own rooms here, she overlooked the desert's sweep.

She rarely left Kourdane, but time was running out.

Every day, every hour was precious to her, every sunrise, every fruit and flower.

When Si Bachir died in 1911, Aurélie was sixty-two and knew that at last her life of love was ended.

Si Bachir's malice reached out from the grave. He had left her nothing — not even a life interest in Kourdane.

The property was automatically inherited by her stepson Si Ali, and he too was jealous of her powerful presence.

Aurélie was thunder-struck.

When he suggested she should take with her anything she chose, her fury was uncontrolled and she refused to leave.

Finally, Si Ali ejected her by law.

After her departure for Algiers, it was found that she had emptied the Palace. Rugs, silver, linen, furniture, bric-a-brac, the bronze chandeliers, the pearl furniture and the grand piano were all piled into wagons and trundled away.

When asked to render the accounts of the *Zaouia* she refused.

For three years she remained in obstinate silence, lodged in a small house into which were crammed the glories of Kourdane.

Three years of this aimless existence dragged by, then once more, for the fourth and last time, Fate stepped in.

And once again, as in the beginning, chance was heralded by gunfire.

In 1914 France was in desperate straits, and when the Germans began fostering revolts in North Africa, the French remembered Lallah Yamina, *Princesse des Sables*.

They sent for her and begged her to return to Ain Mahdi to work for French interests among the tribes.

For six more years the sun shone on her: a sinking sun, but it warmed her through.

Si Ali had become a reformed, if timid Shareef, and, all the old spites forgotten, welcomed her return to Ain Mahdi.

Thus, yet again, the *Princesse des Sables* reigned, to the benefit of the Tedjanis, the furtherance of French interests, and the destruction of German influences.

With the Armistice, Aurélie, at seventy-two, felt her Saharan life must finish. Her wartime efforts had exhausted her.

Even Kourdane seemed too demanding, and she decided to go home to Arc-en-Barrois.

Her money and possessions had long vanished, she was poor and not made welcome by her relatives.

She began to fret for Kourdane — Kourdane and the Sahara.

In 1933, in a surge of the old temerity and resolve, she returned to Algeria.

She made the journey to Ain Mahdi in a rackety tourist bus, she who had first made it at the head of that extravagant marriage cortege.

She sat, an impoverished spectre among the tourists, over eighty, but still a woman in love.

She asked to be allowed to return to Kourdane, and the Tedjanis agreed. Kourdane was of little account to the confraternity now.

Once more she found that the Sahara had claimed its own and Kourdane stood, a lonely ruin.

Emaciated sheep cropped weeds where once her roses had bloomed, the wells had dried up, the desert had crept up smothering everything.

The Tedjanis took her to the *Soeurs Blanches* at El Aghouat.

There, in a small room containing an iron bed an old armchair and a statue of the Virgin Mary, she lay silently.

Sometimes she whispered in Arabic, seeming to relive those wonderful, audacious days of her Saharan beginnings.

The Tedjanis and the Shareefs family came often to see her, all solicitude. The French priest visited her constantly, observing that the worn Bible at her bedside was inscribed with her name.

It had been beside her all these years, a testament to her unchanging faith.

She was failing fast, now, and received the Sacraments, so the next day, she asked to be taken back to Kourdane.

It was a long and terrible route, and the doctor forbade her being moved, but she would not be dissuaded.

"Kourdane — I can only die happy there," they heard her whisper.

The Tedjanis carried her across the desert she had loved to the ruined domain that was still the Pavilion of her heart.

Twenty-four hours later she was dead.

She had wished to be buried there, in a Moslem tomb, beside Si Ahmed, and all the fanaticism of the Tedjanis now rose round her coffin.

They claimed she had been at the end converted to Islam, though this the French disputed hotly, citing her receiving the Sacraments and her treasured Bible.

It was well known that she had never adopted her husband's religion, however much she had become one with the Confraternity.

Therefore, said the French, she must have a Christian burial in the Catholic cemetery at Laghouat.

Such arguments seem trivial in view of her expressed wish to lie at Kourdane.

Yet the wrangling continued, Faith against Faith.

Belatedly the French Government accorded her the

honours they had not bestowed during her life-time, they named her *Chevalier de la Legion d'Honneur* and many more high-sounding titles.

As 'The first French woman of the Sahara' they gave her, beside their usual *pompe funebre,* a funeral with full Military honours, her coffin draped with the *tricolore* and a salvo of guns to echo across the sands.

But the Arabs designated her a *Maraboute,* a Moslem saint, and buried her beside Si Ahmed, under the green vaults of the pistachio tree, surrounded by the desert she had loved so passionately for so long.

PRINCE SI AHMED AND AURÉLIE PICCARD

ACKNOWLEDGEMENTS

Barbara Cartland wishes to thank the following people very much:

Montgomery Hyde, "The Empress Catherine and Prince Dashkov"; Aubrey Richardson, "The Lover of Queen Elizabeth"; Gina Kaus, "Catherine The Great"; Stafan Zweig, "The Queen of Scots"; Eva Scott, "Six Stuart Sovereigns 1512-1701"; Lt.-Col. Andrew C. P. Haggard, "Sidelights on the Court of France"; Count D'Ornano, "Life and Loves of Marie Walewska"; Barbara Cartland, "Book of Beauty and Health"; Sir Herbert Maxwell, "Sixty Years a Queen"; H. K. Prescot, "The Early and Middle Ages"; Edmund d'Auvergne, "A Queen at Bay"; Martin Hume, "The Wives of Henry VIII"; The Illustrated London News 1900 and 1902"; Neville Connell, "Anne"; Octave Aubry, "Eugenie Empress of France"; Baring Gould, "The Tragedy of The Caesars"; P. W. Sergeant, "The Empress Josephine"; Barbara Cartland, "The Outrageous Queen"; Stenton, "William The Conqueror"; Curties, "A Forgotten Prince of Wales"; Fletcher and Kipling, "A History of England"; Choiseul Gouffier, "Alexander I and Court of Russia"; Charles Petrie, "Louis XIV"; Dunn Paterson, "The Black Prince Edward"; Waliszewski, "Ivan The Terrible"; Cornelius Gurhitt, "August de Starke"; Maura Camazo, "Carlos II Su Corte"; Benjamin Ide Wheeler, "Alexander The Great"; G. F. Kunz, "The Book of The Pearl"; Princess Catherine Radziwill, "Sovereigns & Statesmen of Europe"; Lt.-Col. Andrew Haggard, "The Real Louis XV"; Rachel Challice, "Secret History of The Court of Spain"; Michael Senior, "Richard II"; Francoise de Bernardy, "The Princes of Monaco"; C. C. Trench, "The Royal Malady"; Harmsworth Encyclopaedia, Vol. VI; M. W. Freer, "Henry III of France and Poland"; Alfred E. T. Watson, "King Edward VII as a Sportsman"; Barbara Cartland,

"The Fragrant Flower"; Hugh Stokes, "A Prince of Pleasure Philip of France and His Court"; Michael Prawdin, "The Mad Queen of Spain"; Mrs. Bearne, "A Sister of Marie Antoinette"; Graham, "Life of Alexander II"; Jerome Dreifuss, "The Romances of Catherine and Potemkin"; Francis Cribble, "The Royal House of Portugal"; H.R.H. Prince Tomislav of Yugoslavia; Dr. Rappoport, "Leopold II King of The Belgians"; A. Hilliard Atteridge, "Napoleon's Brothers"; Wilson, "Napoleon The Man"; Frederick de Reichenberg, "Prince Metternich in Love and War"; Barbara Cartland, "The Passionate Diplomat"; Barbara Cartland, "Romantic Royal Marriages"; Edward Legge, "King Edward in His True Colours"; Barbara Cartland, "Diane de Poittiers"; "The Coronation of Their Majesties King George VI and Queen Elizabeth"; King Albert's Book"; Sigmund Munz, "King Edward VII at Marienbad"; Walter Jerrold, "Henry VIII and His Wives"; Iain Moncreiffe and Don Pottinger, "Simple Heraldry"; Prince Michael of Greece, "Crown Jewels of Britain and Europe"; Guido Gregorietti, "Jewellery Through The Ages"; S. Baring Gould, M.A., "Farouk of Egypt"; David Randall, "Royal Follies"; Daniel George, "A Book of Characters"; Jean Plaidy, "The Spanish Inquisition"; Joanna Richardson, "La Vie Parisienne"; Anita Leslie, "Edwardians in Love"; Barbara Cartland, "The Outrageous Queen'; Barbara Cartland, "Empress of Austria"; Barbara Cartland, "A Year of Royal Days"; Virginia Cowles, "The Romanovs"; Lesley Blanch, "Wilder Shores of Love"; Barbara Cartland, "Love and Lovers"; Barbara Cartland, "Written With Love"; Nina Epton, "Lovers and the French"; Nina Epton, "Lovers and the English"; E. Barrington, "The Laughing Queen"; Beatrice Clay, "Stories of Arthur and The Round Table"; Joanna Richardson, "The Courtesans"; Nancy Mitford, "The Sun King"; G. F. Kunz, "Curious Law of Precious Stones"; G. F. Kunz, "Magic of Jewels and Charms"; William Jones, "Finger

Ring Lore"; Thomas Secombe, "Twelve Bad Men"; Dorothy Marshall, "Victoria"; Norah Lofts, "Anne Boleyn"; Arthur Vincent, "Twelve Bad Women"; E. F. Benson, "The Kaiser and English Relations"; Longworth, "The Three Empresses"; Erskin, "29 Years of Alfonso XIII of Spain"; Segur, "Marie Antoinette"; Haslip, "Marie Antoinette"; Asprey, "Frederick The Great"; Michael Prestwick, "Edward I"; John Gillingham, "Life and Times of Richard I"; Michael Senior, "Life and Times of Richard II"; Rossabi Khubilia Khan, "Khubilia Khan"; W. B. Henderson, "Life of The Emperor Nero"; Wiegall, "Nero"; R. Davey, "Sultan and His Subjects"; Cronholm, "History of Sweden"; J. S. Orvis, "A Brief History of Poland"; Joan Evans, "Magical Jewels of the Middle Ages and the Renaissance"; Antonia Fraser, "The Kings and Queens of England"; Leslie Field, "The Queen's Jewels"; Maurice Ashley, "The Life and Times of King John"; Princess Michael of Kent, "Crowned in a Far Country"; Nancy Mitford, "Frederick The Great"; Suzy Jerkes, "The Royal Jewels"; Alexander von Solodkoff, "Masterpieces from The House of Fabergé"; John Lord, "The Maharajas"; Lesley Blanch, "Pavilions of The Heart"; Theo Lang, "My Darling Daisy"; Cecil Woodham Smith, "Queen Victoria"; Elizabeth Longford, "Victoria I"; Antonia Fraser, "Mary Queen of Scots"; Debretts Kings and Queens of Europe; David Williamson, Webb & Bower (Michael Joseph); Christine Sutherland, Maria Walenska, Napoleon's Great Loves.

OTHER TITLES CURRENTLY AVAILABLE IN

The Royal Series

ROYAL ECCENTRICS

ROYAL JEWELS

Look out for more titles
in this exciting new series in your
bookshop soon